Greenhouses for longer summers

Heinz and Geneste Kurth

GREENHOUSES

for longer summers

B. T. BATSFORD LTD., LONDON

Acknowledgements: the authors are particularly grateful to **Baco Leisure Products Ltd.**, Huntingdon, England, for their generous help in providing one of the Baco 'Professional' range of greenhouses to assist them with their research, for giving many construction details of their aluminium greenhouses and for demonstrating the method of erecting a typical model. They also thank Peter McHoy for his contributions to the manuscript. Final thanks are due to Jack Budgen and Jack Marshall for their advice on many aspects of greenhouse management.

Other titles in the series
By Heinz and Geneste Kurth
BARBECUE and the joy of cooking on an open fire
OUTDOOR HOLIDAYS for indoor people
WINEMAKING at home
Consultant editor : Ann Lamacraft
RESTORING furnishings for the home

First published in Great Britain in 1982 by B. T. Batsford Limited, 4 Fitzhardinge Street, London W1H 0AH

Created and produced by Ventura Publishing Ltd., 44 Uxbridge Street, London W8 7TG

ISBN 0 7134 4029 5

Filmset by SX Composing Ltd., Rayleigh, Essex
Colour origination by D. S. Colour International Limited, London
Printed in Spain

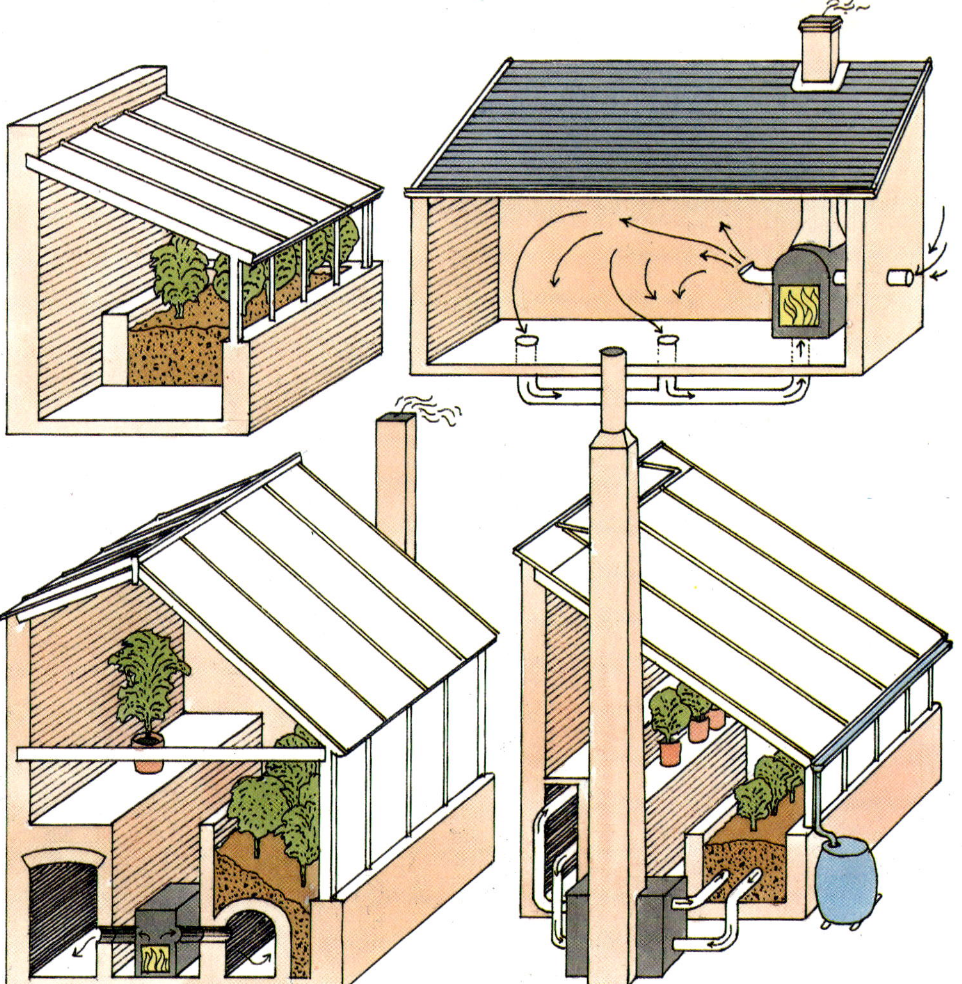

Extra heat allowed plants to be grown earlier and many 'foreign' plants to be cultivated. A warm greenhouse uncontaminated by smoke and exhausted air, however, took a few centuries to be developed.

Top left: *in this 17th Century 'glasshouse', plants in their pots were sunk into a pit filled with tan-bark or dung which gives off heat while fermenting.*
Top right: *fumes from furnaces are not healthy for plants. That is why outside air was heated in pipes first before being led to the plant area in this 17th Century English greenhouse. Contaminated air from the furnace itself was drawn out through holes in the floor by the pull of the fire and stack.*
Lower left: *in the 1810 French greenhouse, hot air and smoke are led through flues located under the plant-beds before being drawn out by the stack.*
Lower right: *by about 1850 many Victorian greenhouses were still warmed by a furnace. But no longer was the heat carried via flues. Instead, an outside furnace heated water in a boiler from which hot water was led to the plant-beds in pipes and returned to be heated again – like modern central heating systems.*

contents

From orangeries to space domes

If man ever colonises the moon, he will probably erect something on the lunar surface which is very much like a greenhouse. He will need to create an enclosed environment where he can live in comfort, surrounded by greenery and protected from the harsher conditions outside – in fact, exactly the same requirements that first led to the development of greenhouses about three hundred years ago.

At that time, the nobility of northern Europe were finding that the natural climate did not suit them, partly because of fashion and partly because the weather seemed to be colder than it had been in previous centuries. So they ordered their builders to construct 'orangeries' in the grounds of their stately homes. These were large, airy rooms adorned and scented by citrus trees where they could sit or stroll in winter and where the ladies would not have their pale complexions ruined by too much vulgar sunlight in the summer.

The orangery built for the Duke of Devonshire at Chatsworth in England was a huge chamber over 262ft (80m) long, 131ft (40m) broad, and rising to a height of about 65ft (20m).

Daniel Defoe records that another famous orangery devised by Wren and Vanburgh for Queen Anne at Hampton Court Palace in 1704 was intended as a Winter Garden but that the Queen 'often was pleased to make the Green House, which is very beautiful, her Summer Supper House'. The same convenience was soon being enjoyed by other great ladies and gentlemen who could afford it, in places as far apart as trendy Paris and Potemkin's imposing Palace of Taurida in St. Petersburg.

Once the idea had caught on, the original palatial buildings were gradually scaled down and given glass roofs so that by 1824 it was said that 'a greenhouse, which fifty years ago was a luxury not often to be met with, is now become an appendage to every villa, and to many town residences'.

By this time, although the 'conservatory' was still a place designed for people rather than for plants, far more than just orange trees were being grown there.

Opposite page: *many orangeries of the 18th Century already had glass fronts and roofs. Early in summer, the exotic trees were carried to the forecourt of the building. Note lugs on the clay urns through which carrying poles could be inserted. Watering the plants was an arduous task since buckets had to be carried by hand.*

Below: *the modern geodesic dome of the 'Climatron' at the Missouri Botanic Gardens. Inside, watering, temperature and humidity are automatically controlled while curtains of air isolate plant-groups imported from different climates.*

The greenhouse was being used more and more for horticultural as well as social purposes.

When the Jardin d'Hiver was constructed in Paris in 1847, and other big cities like Berlin provided their inhabitants with public Winter Gardens, people were able to see and copy the achievements of professional gardeners.

Botanists and local administrators brought back exotic plants from foreign parts and they were put on display in magnificent iron-and-glass structures like the Palm House at Kew Gardens just outside London, designed by Decimus Burton and Richard Turner and begun in 1844. The Palm House was a hothouse in which a high temperature and humidity were maintained all the year round by circulating hot water through pipes from an outside boiler.

What a greenhouse does for you

The development of the greenhouse did not stop in the 19th Century. Modern commercial greenhouses have an environment controlled by computer. Water and nutrients are fed to the plants automatically, light is provided by special fluorescent tubes linked to a timeswitch, and an ideal temperature is maintained by thermostatically-controlled heaters. It is scarcely necessary for a human operative to intervene.

Luckily, for the average gardener there is no need to go quite that far! The most practical greenhouse is a multi-purpose piece of equipment that helps its owner to make better use of his existing garden. It is an up-to-date version of the 19th century glasshouse, perhaps incorporating one or two modern features such as a maintenance-free aluminium alloy framework and automatic ventilation. If electricity is installed, it will probably have an electric propagator, or at least soil-warming cables. The advantage remains the same as it was almost three centuries ago: in effect you make the summer longer.

Even in a greenhouse without any artificial heating, hardy plants can be induced to flower or fruit earlier than they would outside in the garden. At the end of the natural season it may offer sufficient protection from frost to ripen late tomatoes or harvest beans in pots when the crops outside have finished. Used as a giant cloche, an unheated greenhouse will lengthen the growing season by several weeks, wherever you happen to live.

A greenhouse also makes it possible for you to grow 'guest-plants' that come originally from a warmer climate and will not thrive out of doors in cooler regions. Gardenias, for example, are colourful scented flowers that bloom naturally in China but which can be cultivated only with the help of a greenhouse in most parts of northern Europe.

If your family derives enjoyment from gardenias and other flowers such as freesias, gloxinias, and lemon-scented pelargoniums, it is becoming more and more expensive to fill the house with these by buying them from the local florist or garden centre. But with a heated greenhouse you can easily grow these and many other indoor plants.

From one packet of coleus seed, for instance, you can produce masses of decorative foliage. With many plants you can also take cuttings and fill your home and garden with lovely flowering plants for a very small outlay.

Equally important, for many people, is the possibility of growing fruit and vegetables out of season. It is quite feasible to supply your family and friends with fresh, crisp lettuces when the price is high and the quality not so dependable in greengrocers'. As the days lengthen and grow warmer, you can also begin to sow seeds for cucumbers, courgettes, and melons. And, of course, there are tomatoes to be grown. If you can provide enough warmth early in the year you can be picking tomatoes by the end of June. Even if your crops are ripe a bit later, when the price in the shops is coming down, there is always the satisfaction of having grown your own. Tomatoes from the shop seldom have the same taste and tang as those freshly picked from the greenhouse.

In time the greenhouse can actually save you money, but it must be exploited to the full if you expect financial returns from it. For most of us, however, it is the pleasure it brings that is ample reward. The greenhouse is a small private domain where, even in the dormant wintertime, the keen gardener can continue to potter about among his plants. Even the elderly and frail can enjoy greenhouse gardening, since everything can be grown on staging and shelves, with no hard digging or stooping.

The ideal greenhouse

Greenhouses come in so many shapes and sizes, and in such a variety of materials, that choosing which to buy is never easy. The following considerations will help to make the choice a little less confusing.

WHAT DO YOU WANT TO GROW?

If you are keen on growing vegetable crops like cucumbers, melons, tomatoes, and lettuces, it would be best to select a glass-to-ground greenhouse for maximum light. If pot plants are your hobby, then go for a half-timbered greenhouse as wood retains heat well and will be more economical to heat. You will also have room under the staging for shade-loving plants.

If you want to keep your options open because you are not sure what you want to grow, you might consider one half-timbered on one side and glazed to the ground on the other.

HOW MUCH DO YOU WANT TO GROW?

The size of your greenhouse is another important factor. Once you have made the decision about how much space you need you can work out which greenhouse will give you the best value. Bear in mind that the proportion of path to growing space can be important. Calculate the length and breadth of the greenhouse of your choice, excluding paths. If you intend to grow crops where height is important, take into consideration the height to the eaves as well as to the ridge.

HOW MUCH CAN YOU AFFORD?

In these days of inflation when money seems to buy less every year, it would be more expensive in the long run if you were to buy too small a greenhouse which would soon become overcrowded. But if price dictates that you have to start by buying a small one, it is better to select a type that can be extended later. Check whether this is possible.

Next, consider what are usually called the 'optional extras', but which are often 'essentials'. Often bases are extra, though some greenhouses do come with an integral base, so it is worth considering this when comparing prices. Staging is, of course, essential unless you want to confine yourself to border crops, and it can be bought in many forms and lengths for self-assembly to suit all greenhouses (see page 36). There must also be sufficient ventilators, and it may be worth paying for an extra one. It is a good idea to buy a louvred ventilator for one of the sides. Again, some greenhouses come already supplied with these.

Another consideration that may have a bearing on the cost is whether you are going to erect it yourself, or let a reputable builder or specialist employed by the manufacturer do the job. But bear in mind that in some countries, such as Britain, tax arrangements may offset much of the cost of having the supplier carry out the work – assuming you have prepared the site.

HOW DURABLE SHOULD IT BE?

If you have young children around, it might be safer to choose a plastic greenhouse (see page 13). This should last for a couple of years and can serve later as a giant cloche in the vegetable garden.

A wood-framed greenhouse, on the other hand, is a permanent structure if it is erected on a brick base. There are, however, aluminium alloy, and some wood-framed, greenhouses that can be dismantled and re-erected with relative ease. They can be unbolted from their bases of pre-cast concrete or aluminium. This feature may be useful if you want to move to a new district, or when after a few years your garden layout alters – or a neighbour's overhanging tree has grown to fantastic heights. Do not forget that moving them can be time-consuming and quite fiddly, so try to make sure you site your greenhouse correctly in the first place.

SEEKING ADVICE

One of the best ways to find out about potential snags and problems, which the sales leaflets will not tell you, is to ask friends or neighbours who already have a greenhouse. Ask them to show you round and they will very soon point to features or equipment that they found useful, and those items that did not come up to the promised standard. Armed with this information, visit a few garden centres, which usually have a wide range of greenhouses on display. When your mind is almost made up, do not hesitate to contact the manufacturer to assure yourself about details that may not be clearly explained in their brochure.

TYPES AND MATERIALS

The basic choice for the framework of any glazed greenhouse is either wood or aluminium alloy.

Wood expands and contracts to some extent according to the weather, so its glass panes have to be mounted flexibly, using putty or a mastic. Wood also needs to be painted or treated with preservative regularly.

Aluminium alloy is sometimes offered with a coating of enamel or acrylic paint, which adds to the appearance of the structure. On untreated aluminium, a certain amount of harmless corrosion takes place when it is first exposed to the weather. This appears as a white powdery deposit, which dulls the surface, but does not weaken the material itself – unlike steel which will rapidly rust if it is not protected.

Galvanised tubular steel is usually used for plastic greenhouses because it is strong and yet can easily be bent into hoops. Galvanised steel has a long life if handled carefully, but any suspect areas should be treated at once with a rust-proofer.

Doorways can be a problem, so if you want to bring in barrowloads of plants or compost, make sure that the opening is wide enough for your wheelbarrow, and that the base of the doorway is flush with the ground or has a ramp.

There are hinged single or double doors and sliding single or double doors to choose from.

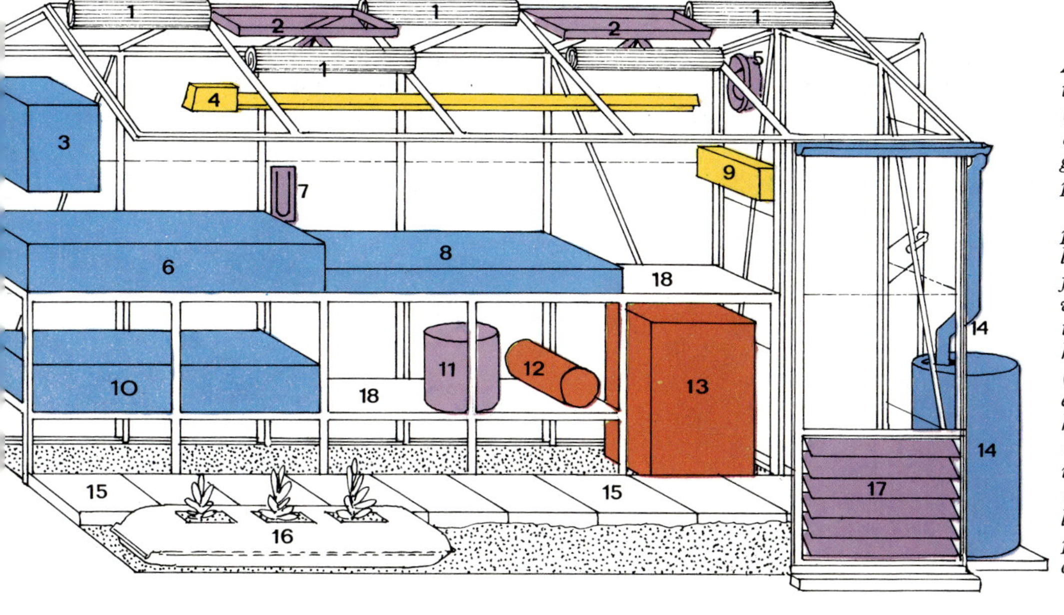

A basic 'starter-kit' might consist of: two-tiered staging (18); roof vents (2); louvred wall ventilators (17); a min/max thermometer (7); guttering and water butt (14) and a paraffin or gas heater (13).

But if you are out most of the day, pre-set automatic systems described later would allow your greenhouse to function unattended: control panel with time switches linked to thermostats for water, heat and humidity (9); automatic roof vents (2); automatic wall vents (17); extractor fan (5); electric blow-heater/cooler (12); header tank (3); mist propagator (6); trickle irrigation (10); capillary matting (8); humidifier (11); fluorescent light (4); external blinds (1); paved path (15) and growing-bags on border soil (16).

Wood

Some greenhouses are made from teak or oak, but western red cedar is the wood most widely used for timber-framed greenhouses. Red cedar is particularly rot proof and, provided it has been impregnated with a good preservative, it will only need painting inside and out with a wood preservative – or, even better, linseed oil – once every three or four years. Many gardeners prefer this type of greenhouse because it blends with the garden far better than one made of a bright alloy.

Because wood is not as strong as metal, timber sections have to be rather thick, which cuts down a certain amount of light, but as wood absorbs and retains more heat, it is possible that a timber-framed greenhouse will be warmer than an alloy one as the evenings cool. This difference may not be great, however, as most heat will be lost through the glass.

Timber should not have any direct contact with the soil, so the frame must be erected on a brick or concrete base. Even wooden staging inside the greenhouse should be mounted on bricks. If these precautions are taken, a timber-framed greenhouse will last for many years.

Wood is easy to drill when you need to fit wire supports, shelves, and hooks. It is also easy to line with plastic for winter insulation, using drawing-pins. You can, however, buy fittings to use with an aluminium greenhouse.

Aluminium

Aluminium alloy, bare or enamelled, is now the most popular framework for greenhouses. It is light, strong, and needs virtually no maintenance. The frame-members are strong and have narrow glazing bars, so allowing most of the available light to enter during the winter months. The sections are usually easy to erect and are simply bolted together. Some types have an integral base, others rest on precast concrete sections, or on a separate aluminium base. An added bonus is that many of the structures come complete with condensation channels running along the inside under the eaves, and inner grooves where shelves and plant supports can be attached. With a

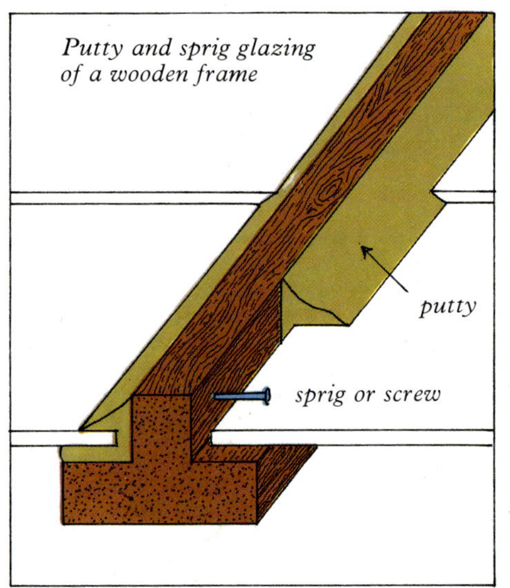

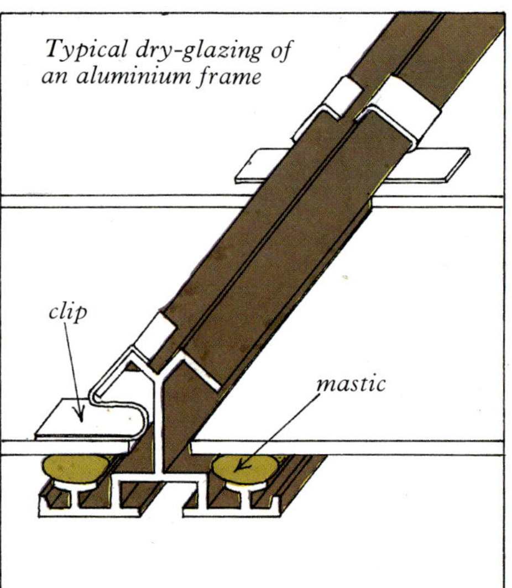

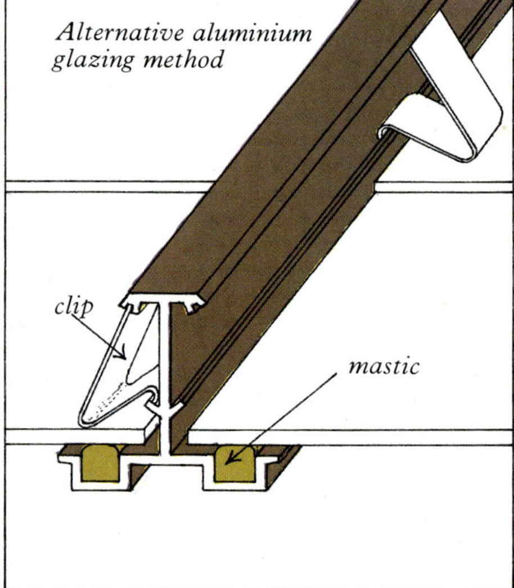

modern aluminium greenhouse you should not need to drill holes as special bolts and clips are readily available if you want to add shelves or insulation.

Metal is a conductor of cold and heat, and these houses may cool a little more rapidly than wooden ones But there is better light in winter because of the narrower frames and glazing bars.

Glazing an aluminium-framed greenhouse is much simpler than glazing a timber-framed house; instead of nails and putty, the panes of glass are simply bedded onto mastic or plastic glazing strips and securely clipped into position. Glazing is best done on a calm day, and if at all possible, it should be finished by the evening since a half completed greenhouse is vulnerable and may be damaged if a strong wind springs up.

Plastic

Plastic greenhouses are light, portable structures that are cheap, easy to erect, and safer than glass if there are children around.

The basic framework is usually tubular alloy or galvanised steel, but should not be constructed from a mixture of both.

Even 600-gauge polythene treated with an ultraviolet inhibitor (UVI) has a relatively short life and will probably need renewal every two or three years. Plastic tends to become yellow and brittle with age, is easily scratched, and because of its electrostatic properties attracts dust which will further diffuse the light. Long-wave solar radiation is not trapped inside a plastic greenhouse, so it will cool more rapidly than a glass structure.

Condensation is a major problem, and it tends to drip on to the plants instead of running down the sides.

Firm anchorage is essential with all polythene greenhouses.

There are clear PVC greenhouses available, and these do have a longer life, but still lack many of the qualities of a glass greenhouse.

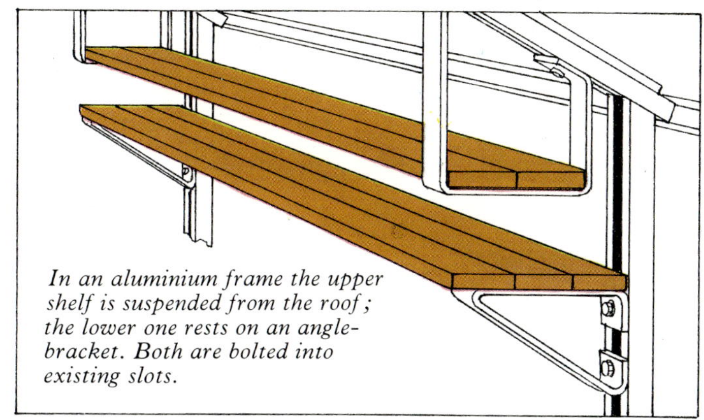

In an aluminium frame the upper shelf is suspended from the roof; the lower one rests on an angle-bracket. Both are bolted into existing slots.

Staging and extra shelves are easily fitted to a wooden frame.

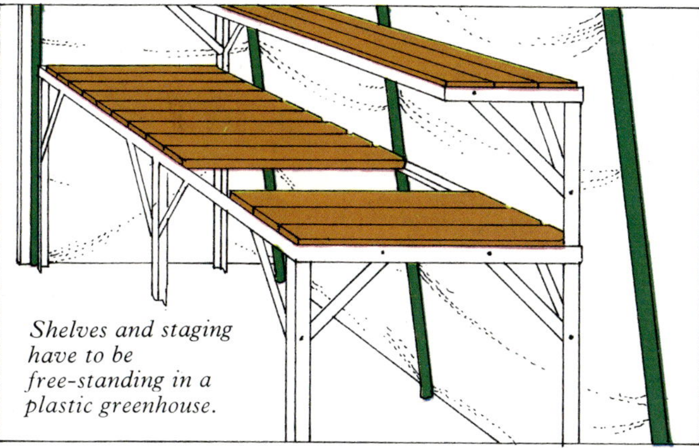

Shelves and staging have to be free-standing in a plastic greenhouse.

Basic greenhouse shapes

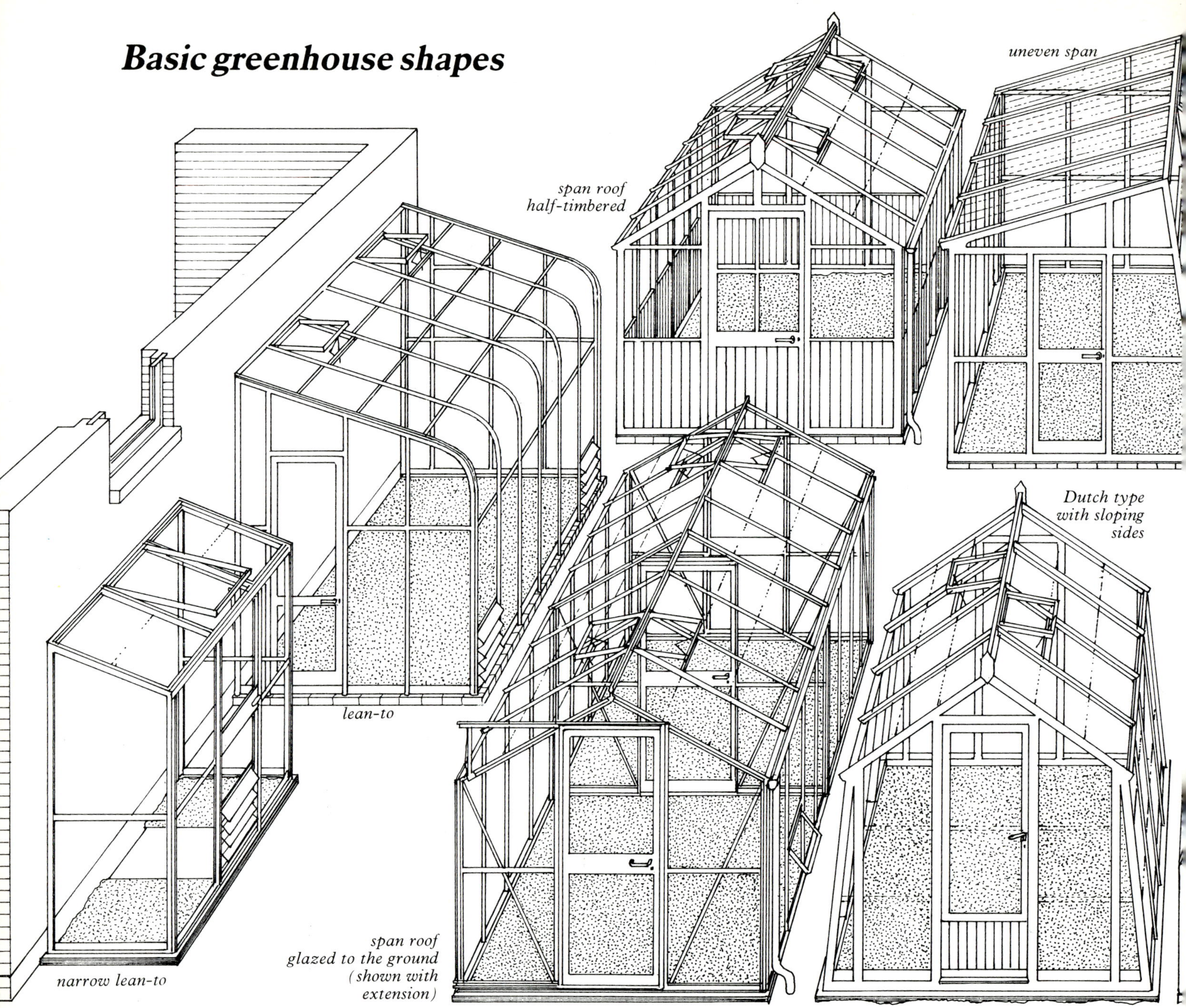

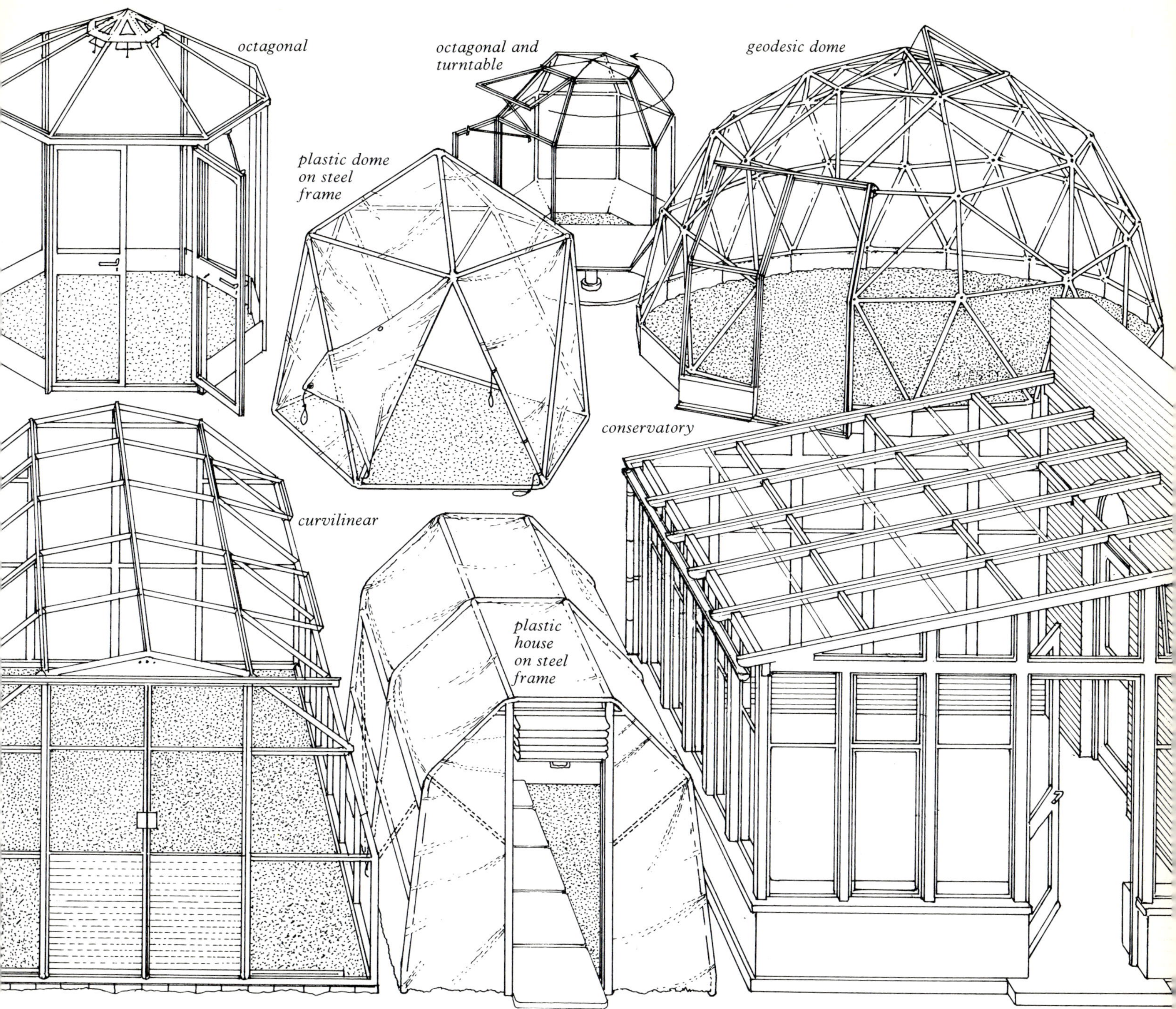
octagonal
octagonal and
turntable
geodesic dome
plastic dome
on steel
frame
conservatory
curvilinear
plastic
house
on steel
frame

Span-roofed houses

In span-roofed houses, the pitched roof rises to a central ridge with both sides of the roof of equal size (except in the uncommon three-quarter-span type). Where the glass panes overlap, the roof tends to have a steeper pitch than those of the unlapped type like the Dutch design.

Too shallow an incline could possibly cause problems if you live in a district that has a high snowfall, if the house is not heated.

Dutch houses

The sloping sides of this type usually have larger panes of glass. Its shape allows good light penetration, making it particularly useful for tomatoes, lettuces, and chrysanthemums. Unfortunately, the cost of replacing a broken glass pane would be considerably higher than for a greenhouse with small panes.

The height to the eaves and central ridge may be a bit restricted with this type of greenhouse, but this can be overcome by placing the structure on a higher brick base wall.

Curvilinear houses

These give good light transmission, the roof being gently curved and the individual sections of glass set at roughly 90 degrees to the sun for maximum solar radiation if orientated east to west. Shading in the summer is very necessary, but this is an excellent shape for winter work.

Lean-to houses

Where the only space is a balcony or a small patio, a lean-to is probably the only answer, with the added advantage that water, warmth from the domestic heating system and electricity are all at hand.

Lean-to greenhouses come in many shapes and sizes, and can be made of wood, aluminium alloy, or plastic. The staging and shelving can be free-standing or attached to the back wall. If the back wall is painted white, it will reflect and bounce back a large amount of light – particularly in the winter months.

A south-facing wall will absorb much radiation from the sun with the result that it tends to heat up rapidly in high summer, so shading is important, and a fan ventilator will be useful to moderate temperatures.

The back wall will retain much of the heat and this is gradually released overnight, which may help to raise the temperature a few degrees during the winter. For these reasons, a west-facing lean-to is, on the whole, the best choice. It will provide shade at the peak time of day, yet benefit from the evening sun. A north-facing wall is constantly in shade, so a greenhouse sited here is best devoted to growing ferns or shade-loving plants, and for overwintering fairly hardy plants.

'Circular' and octagonal houses

These decorative structures look attractive, do not take up much space, and can accommodate a surprising number of plants. A disabled gardener may find some benefit in the compact layout.

Although these greenhouses are more expensive than conventionally shaped houses, light and solar heat transmission is excellent.

Geodesic domed houses

The triangular panes and glazing bars make this space-age house not only very attractive but also structurally strong and roomy with a large amount of light entering at many angles. Some of the triangular panes of glass form windows for ventilation, and you may find the large doorway useful.

Choosing the best site

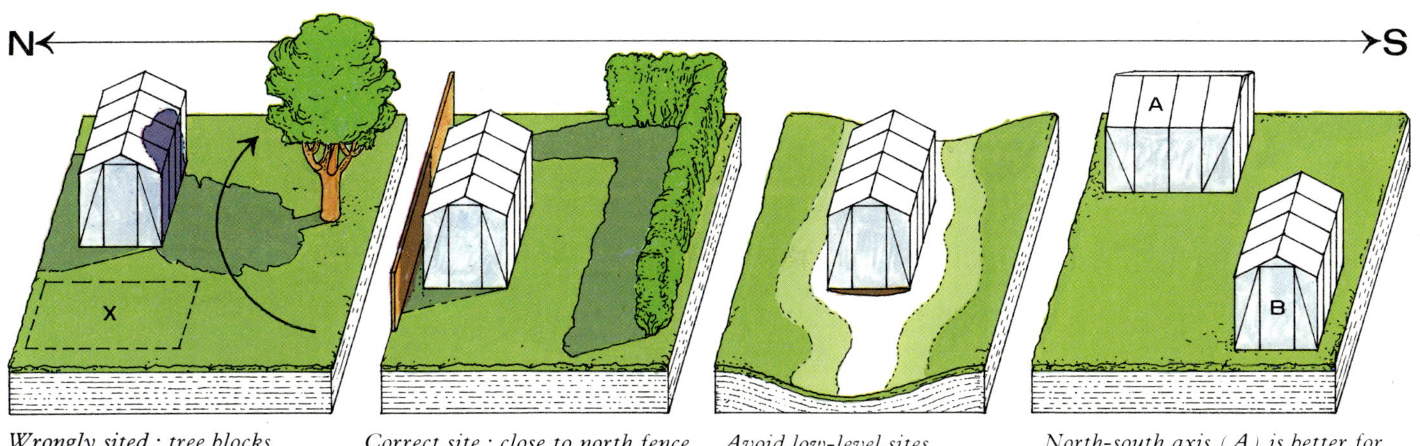

Wrongly sited : tree blocks midday sun. A better site would be at X.

Correct site : close to north fence but far enough away from the east/south hedge. The hedge offers wind protection.

Avoid low-level sites where damp and frost may gather.

North-south axis (A) is better for summer/autumn crops…
… east-west axis (B) produces better winter/spring crops.

The correct placing of a greenhouse in the garden is important. If you are unable to provide the ideal situation, do at least try to choose one that will best suit most of your plants.

LIGHT

If the greenhouse is placed well away from overhanging trees, it will not be affected by falling leaves, which would clog up the gutters, or by falling branches that could break the glass. As all trees shed dirt, this will build up on the glass, cutting out more and more light.

Much trouble can be avoided by not siting it too close to a wall (unless, of course, it is a lean-to), fence or hedge, which would cast shadows and cut out the low-angled winter sun.

If you are planning to cultivate crops in winter or early spring, the ridge of the greenhouse should ideally run from east to west to admit maximum winter light, but for summer and autumn crops, the ridge can run north to south for an equal distribution of light to both sides of the greenhouse. However, as you are likely to grow plants the year round, and the benefits may be marginal, this should not be a major consideration.

SHELTER

Trees are beautiful, but their foliage unfortunately produces shadows. Shadows are also created by buildings, fences, garden walls, and hedges. As all these obstructions are likely to have different heights, it is sometimes difficult to find a spot that remains clear throughout the day.

On the other hand, gardens that are devoid of any shelter are also windy places. And a strong, cold wind that blows across the glass of a greenhouse will cause a considerable loss of heat. In such a situation you may be prepared to plant a hedge or erect a fence as a form of windbreak (but preferably not a solid wall).

Integrated bases are placed straight on level ground. Some have stakes at each corner which have to be embedded in concrete plugs.

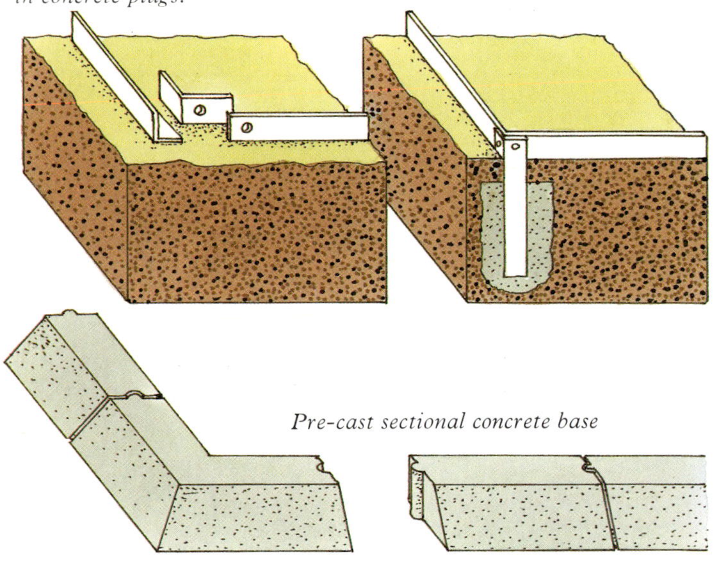

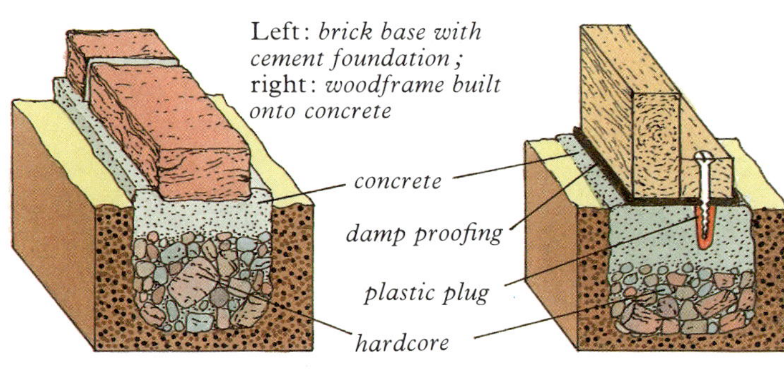

Pre-cast sectional concrete base

Left: *brick base with cement foundation;* right: *woodframe built onto concrete*

Concrete base can simply be cast into a dug trench.

LEVELLING THE CHOSEN SITE

Once the ideal location has been found, the site itself may need some preparation to make it firm, level, and adequately drained. If you want to make a concrete or brick foundation, first level the site and then dig out the trenches, making sure that the area is level by using a spirit-level.

Some greenhouses have an integral base and need only to be erected on level ground. It is important to make sure that the base is correctly squared and level, otherwise the glass panes will not fit properly when you start to glaze.

Other greenhouses constructed of wood or aluminium alloy are mounted on a plinth supplied by the manufacturer. If it is a concrete base, all that is needed is to bolt the individual units together and to check the level before erecting the framework.

Staple underground cables to the underside of creosoted planks. Make a drawing of their location and depth.

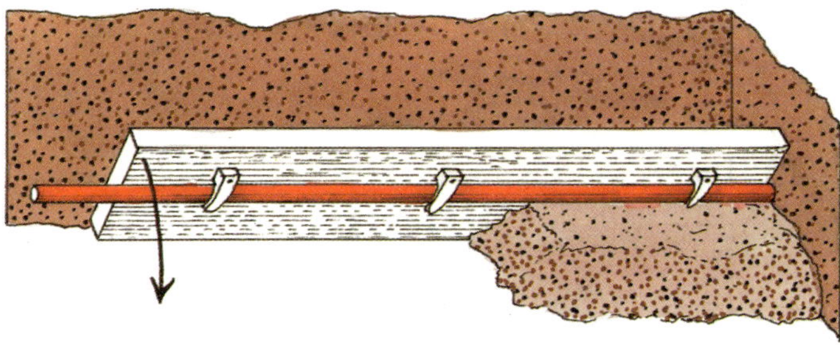

Place bricks over underground water pipes for protection. Pipes and cables should be buried at least 60cm deep.

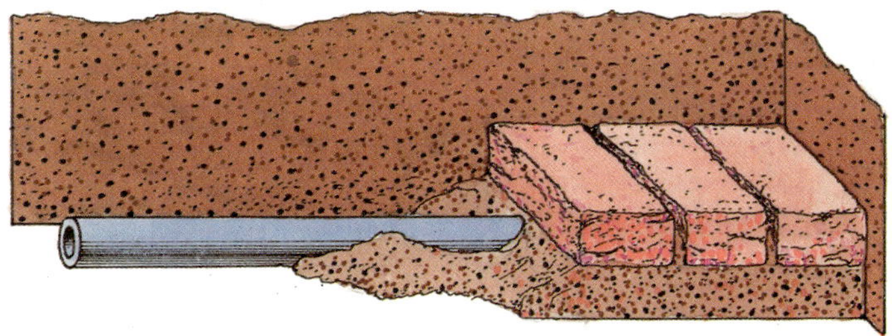

Many aluminium alloy greenhouses are supplied with a matching base with stout metal stakes on each corner for good anchorage. Lay the frame on the marked area and dig out the four holes, unless the instructions advise otherwise. Use a spirit-level and remove any soil that is in the way. Check again that everything is level before packing concrete into the holes to reach just below the soil surface. Allow the concrete to set before filling in the holes and erecting the greenhouse (unless the instructions tell you to fix it to the base before lifting into position).

DRAINAGE

Water, which is so vital to the growth of any plant, can become a nuisance when there is too much of it, or when it collects in the wrong places. So good drainage is essential – not many people like to stand on damp soil in the greenhouse, apart from the fact that during winter the interior should be as dry as possible to avoid condensation and high humidity.

If you have to choose a rather damp site, or if your garden slopes, something has to be done to ensure that rainwater on the ground can be led away from the greenhouse base. Rainwater from the gutters should be collected in water butts. If there are no gutters, make sure there is adequate drainage to prevent the surrounding soil from becoming waterlogged.

SERVICES

Now – before you erect the greenhouse – is the best time to consider the benefits of having piped water and electricity laid on, as the entry points should ideally be planned before the greenhouse base is placed in position. Both electricity and water supplies will have to be connected to your existing domestic systems, a job best left to a qualified craftsman whose standards of work will satisfy any regulations governing the supply.

Because it is more expensive to run a supply to a distant part of the garden, you may want to consider this aspect when siting the greenhouse.

Water

A small-bore supply pipe will suffice for most amateur gardeners' needs. If mist propagation or some of the trickle irrigation systems are being contemplated, a larger pipe of at least 1in (25mm) diameter will be needed to produce sufficient volume and pressure. You can, of course, use trickle systems that do not depend on mains pressure.

Metal pipes should be laid in trenches at least 2ft (60cm) deep to avoid a freeze-up in winter; plastic pipes are less affected by frost.

The simplest way of supplying your greenhouse with water is probably already to hand: it is the garden hose, which can temporarily be connected to an outside tap. It will need to be drained completely before the onset of winter so that the frost does not damage it.

Electricity

Electricity in the greenhouse allows the busy gardener to use many types of lighting and propagating equipment, soil-warming cables, heating, watering and ventilating aids.

Because special fittings and conductors are required for outdoor use, it is best to let a specialist advise you. He will also be aware of the various regulations that apply, which may vary from country to country. If you do want to tackle the job yourself after seeking advice, you may have to go to an electrical contractor (not an ordinary electrical shop) for the materials.

Earth-leakage circuit breakers should be incorporated into the system for safety.

It is worth keeping a plan of the exact location of any water pipes and electricity cables, which will prove useful should you later want to alter the garden layout, or when handing over the house and garden to a new owner.

Putting the greenhouse together

1 *Carefully study the manufacturer's instructions. Some systems may differ from the sequence shown here, but most progress in similar stages. Unwrap all the greenhouse components except the glass. Check that the listed items are complete.*

2 *Mark, level and rake the chosen site.*

3 *Assemble the base with its stakes (or bolt the concrete sections together). Dig a hole at each corner for the stakes. Check with a spirit level that the completed base is level.*

4 *Mix 1 part cement, 3 parts sand, 4 parts gravel or shingle with a little water and pour the concrete into the holes keeping the mixture about 8cm below the surface. When set, the concrete forms a solid foundation for your greenhouse.*

5 *On flat ground nearby, assemble the four wall sections. Staging, shelves and ventilators may require fixing nuts which should now be slid into their channels where they can be temporarily held in place with a blob of mastic.*

6 *You may need help to avoid the sections of the framework from flexing as you clamp them to the base.*

7 *Fit the ridge bar and the roof struts.*

8 *Attach the door and any other extra fittings you have chosen. Your framework is complete. If it is a windy day, stop and give it a rest.*

9 *Glazing should be done on a windless day and in one session since a half-glazed greenhouse acts like a sail and may be damaged. Start with the windward bottom panes. Brush off any grit and make sure that the glazing grooves are dry. Place strips of preshaped mastic along the grooves. In cold weather, keep the mastic indoors for a while to make it supple.*

10 *Wear thick gloves when you unwrap the glass panes. Special clips will hold each individual pane in place. The higher pane always overlaps the lower one.*

11 *Glaze the roof in the same way. Your greenhouse is ready to receive its first plants.*

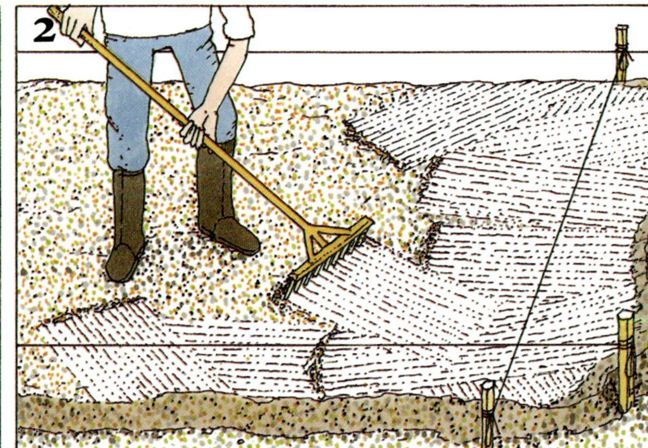

5
6
7
8
9
mastic
10
spring-clip
11

Plants need warmth – heating

THE SUN – HOW IT HEATS THE GREENHOUSE *Short*-wave solar radiation from the sun enters through the glass into the greenhouse where everything it touches such as the floor, staging, plants and pots, heats up. These in turn radiate heat in the form of *long* waves, which do not pass out through the glass.

Even on dull days, a certain amount of short- and long-wave radiation will be present. To make the most of it, the glass panes should be cleaned thoroughly before winter. The cleaner the glass is, the more light will pass through and the higher will be the temperature inside the greenhouse.

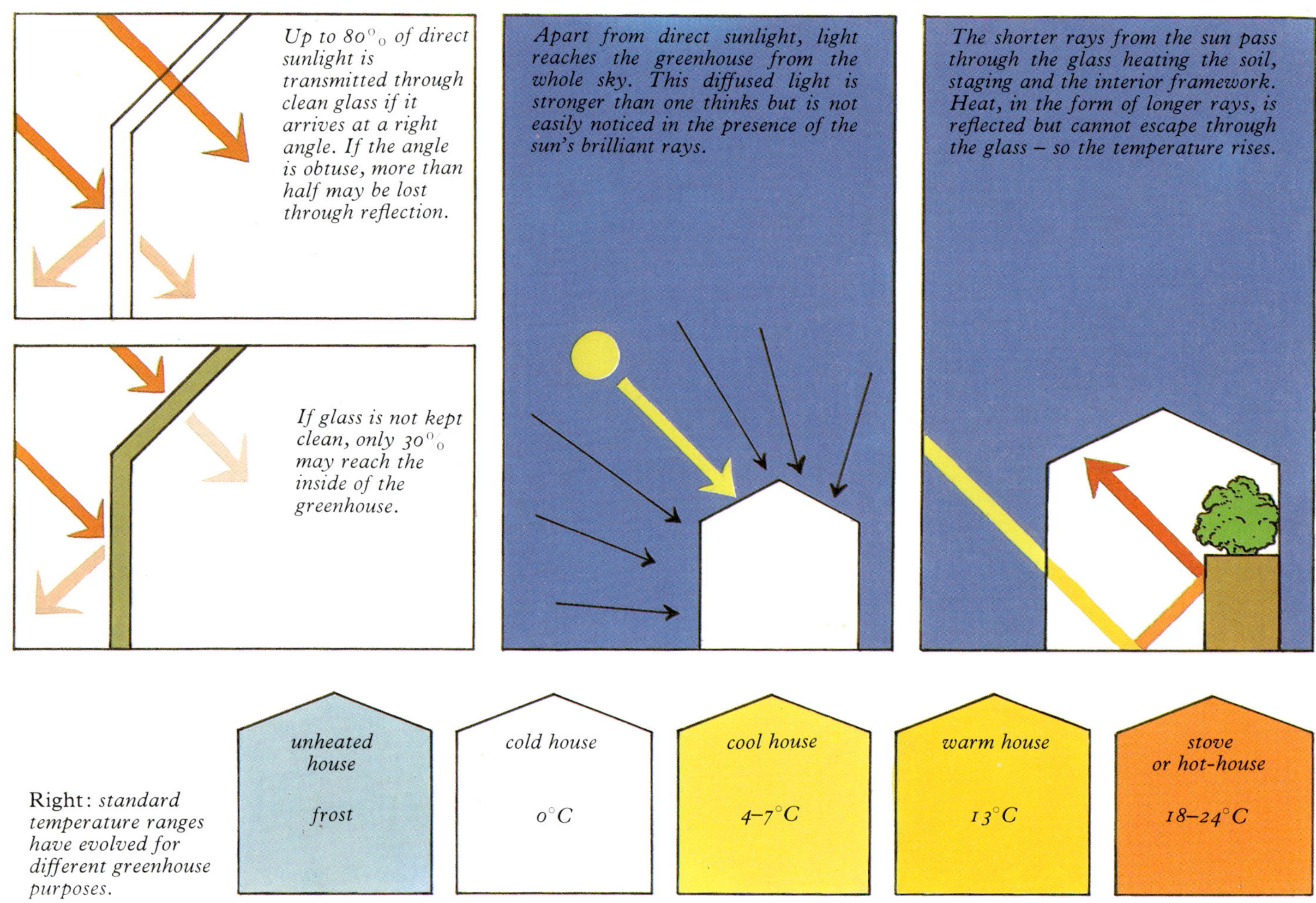

Right: *standard temperature ranges have evolved for different greenhouse purposes.*

PARAFFIN HEATERS

These little stoves provide, at present, the cheapest form of heat if you are trying to keep a reasonably small greenhouse frostproof. They are ideal as a first purchase and the money is not wasted since they can be used when more elaborate heaters fail (during power cuts for instance). Buying the fuel may be inconvenient if the nearest garage or shop is far away.

Make sure that the wick of your paraffin heater is kept well adjusted. If the burner is not kept scrupulously clean, and the wick well trimmed, you may find soot covering your precious plants due to the burning of charred carbon ends.

Once you have made paraffin your main heat source, it is necessary to keep a sharp eye on the level of fuel both in the stove and the reserve supply. If the flame goes out, your plants could suffer badly.

When a paraffin heater is burning, it is wise to have a ventilator open a crack, unless the weather is very severe, to provide sufficient air for proper combustion of the fuel and to allow any potentially harmful fumes to escape. Paraffin produces water vapour and carbon dioxide when it burns. The carbon dioxide is beneficial to plants, the water vapour is not – especially during the winter.

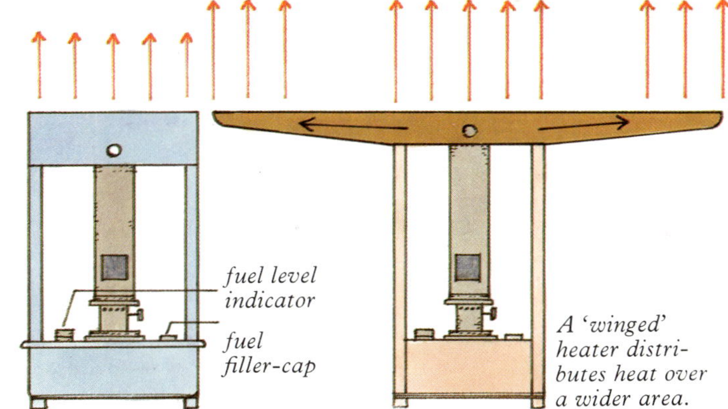

A 'winged' heater distributes heat over a wider area.

If there is a choice between different makes of heaters, there is less risk of fumes being emitted by so-called blue-flame heaters. These have a better air supply to the burner than yellow-flame heaters, and oxidise the fuel more efficiently.

It is worth buying additional pipes or ducts if you own a large greenhouse, to distribute the heat more evenly. Some paraffin heaters are supplied with humidity troughs; to fill with water to give off water vapour; as paraffin heaters already produce water vapour they are best left alone.

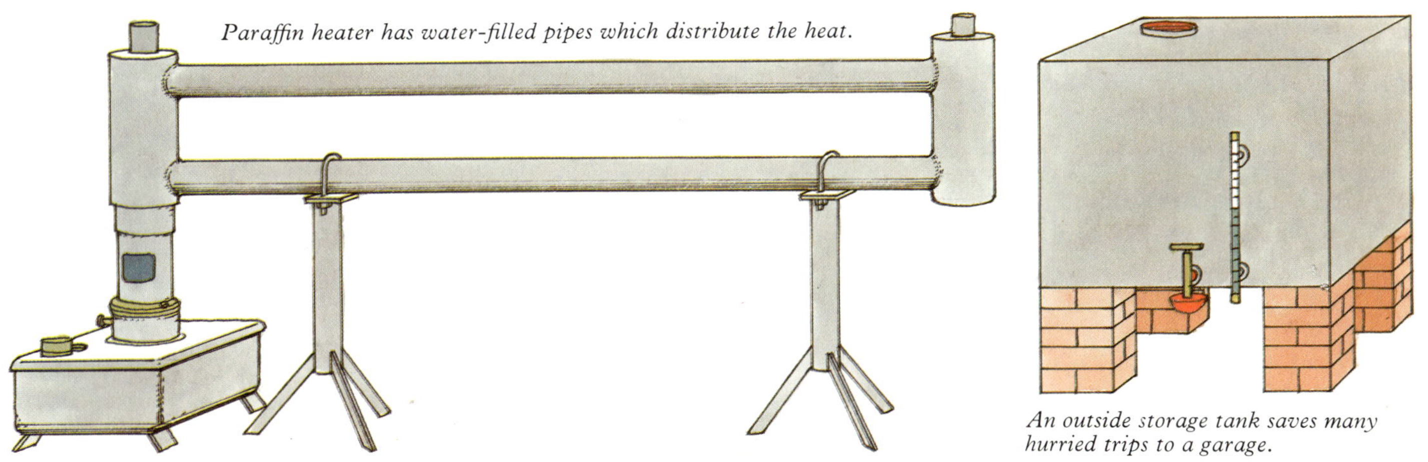

Paraffin heater has water-filled pipes which distribute the heat.

An outside storage tank saves many hurried trips to a garage.

GAS – PIPED AND BOTTLED

If your greenhouse is near the house, or you have added a lean-to, the domestic heating system could possibly be used. Do not be tempted to run an extra radiator from your central-heating system if you are likely to have the system turned off at night. You might be warmly tucked up in bed, but the plants will not be.

If the site is some considerable distance from the house it could be an expensive business laying gas pipes (a job that should only be done by a professional). In this situation, it would probably be cheaper to use bottled gas.

Piped gas

If you want gas to be piped to your greenhouse, you could cut the costs by digging the trench yourself and laying the pipes along it – but it must be done to certain specifications. A professional will then connect the ends, a job you should never attempt yourself.

Bottled gas

Bottled gas provides a convenient form of heating, but the bottle (a pressurised canister) has to be carried; it can be heavy. It is always cheaper to buy a large bottle and to have one as a stand-by that can be connected with an automatic change-over device. This avoids the need to cut off the supply when swapping bottles and is some insurance against running out of gas unexpectedly.

In all cases, when gas burns it gives off carbon dioxide and water vapour, so good ventilation is essential to keep the condensation under control. Most gas heaters need little maintenance.

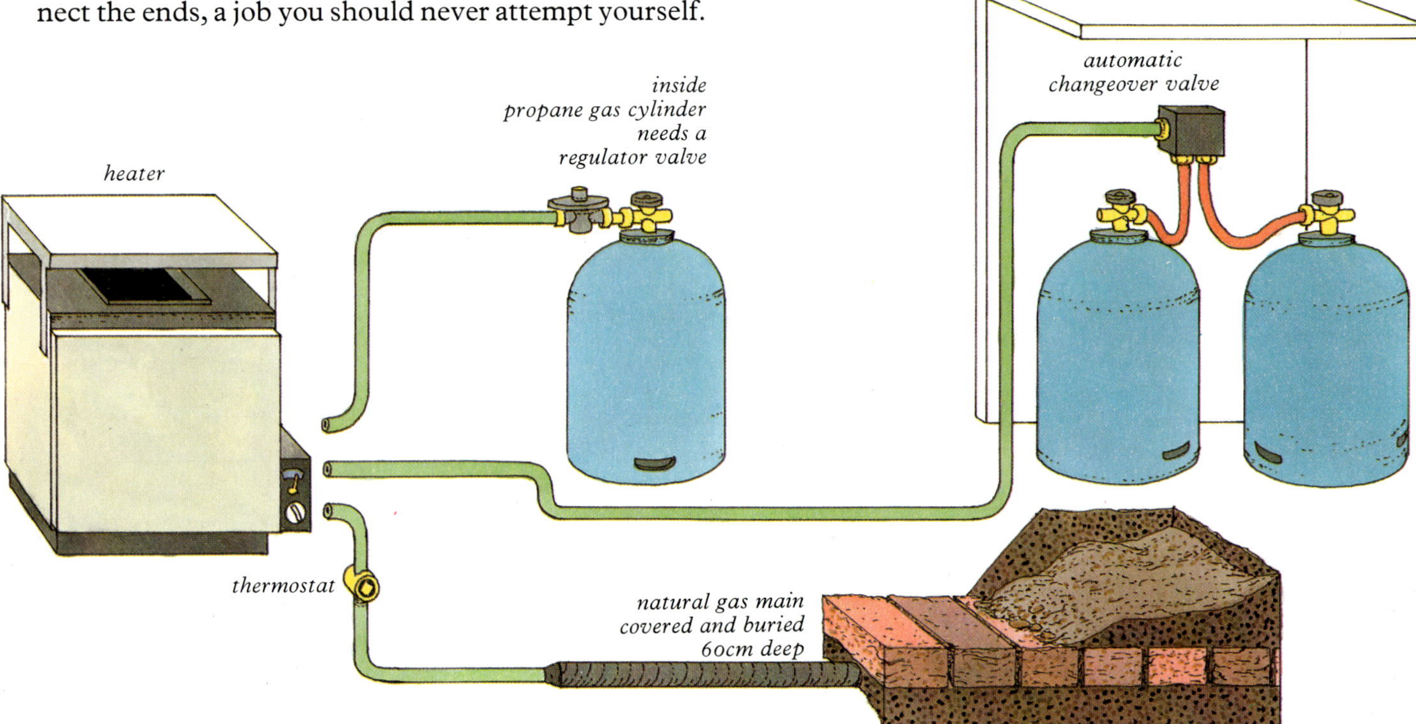

ELECTRICITY

Electricity is the most efficient fuel, but can be the most expensive. On the other hand it is reliable, clean, and very convenient. If you have no readily available source by the chosen site, it is worth having it laid, though this is a fairly costly business. Do get a few estimates from qualified electricians before buying a heater . . . just in case you change your mind.

The cables used, whether above or below ground, *must* be correctly insulated, as should the special waterproof sockets. If more than one socket is needed, have a control panel fitted, which can carry as many powerpoints as you want and has a mains on/off switch. Then it will only be a matter of checking once a year to see that all is in working order.

The advantages of using electricity are numerous. There is no fuel to hump up the garden path on a cold, wet day; strip lighting can be installed for working late on winter evenings; soil-warming cables can be used in the border or in propagators on the staging to rear early seedlings or to root cuttings. Fan heaters with thermostatic control can ensure that the air is dry during the winter, and with warm air blowing about, there will be fewer cold spots. During the hot summer months, the heater can be set to blow cold air around the interior to help ventilation.

Later, extractor fans, mist propagators, and special growing lamps can be added. Apart from fan heaters, there are tubular heaters, often used in 'banks'. These are hollow tubes containing heating elements and should be mounted either along the sides of the greenhouse or on either side of the central path under the staging.

Convector heaters are cabinets containing heating elements for warming the air. The cool air is drawn in at the bottom, heats up as it passes the elements and rises out of the top. Air is kept moving and reduces the problem of cold spots.

The majority of fan heaters have three switches to give a selection of 1kw, 2kw or 3 kw loadings according to the size of your greenhouse. Where possible, select a heater with a rod-type thermostat.

Do not use domestic electrical equipment in a greenhouse. It is NOT safe in wet and humid conditions.

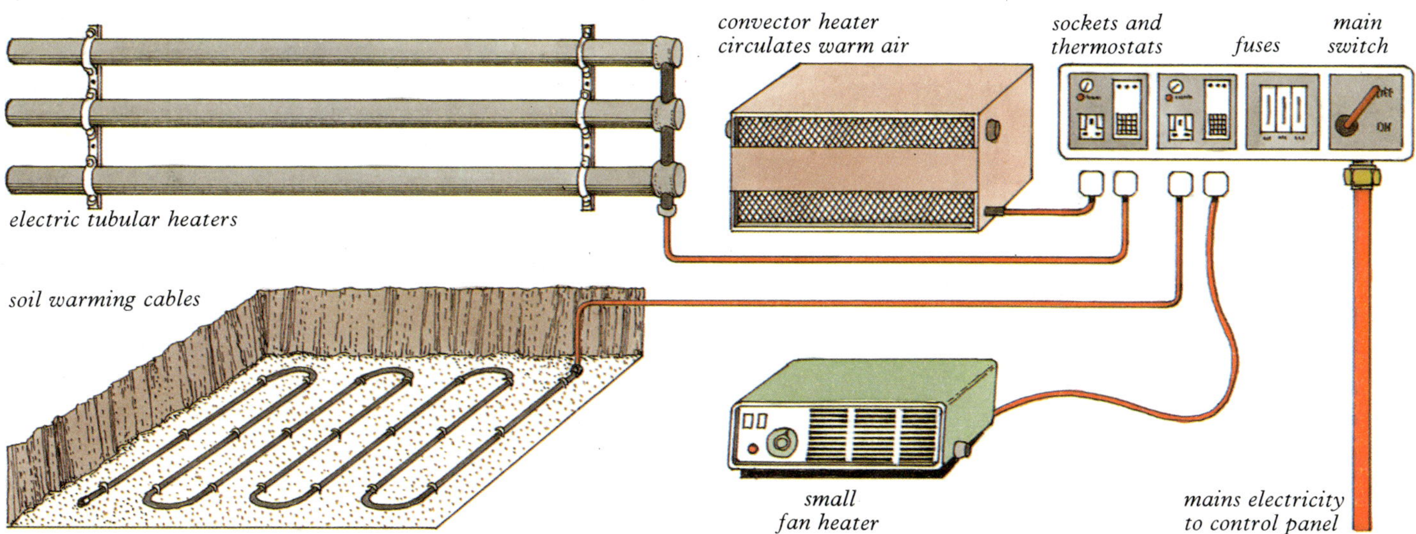

INSULATION

Having made up your mind that you want to heat the greenhouse, or perhaps part of it, and having spent money on a heating installation, you will want to try to conserve as much of the warmth as you can.

Badly fitting doors and vents, or a crack in a glass pane, will let in unwanted cold air. As a result, your fuel bills may rise dramatically so it is vital to deal with the problem *before* winter arrives. And a first step, before insulating your greenhouse, is to make sure that all the glass is really clean so that the maximum amount of light can enter.

Some glass-to-ground greenhouse manufacturers supply tailor-made insulating panels made of wood, asbestos, or rigid plastic. They are easily fixed into position, and once the weather starts to warm up can be removed and stored in a safe place.

A 'thermal screen' (which is a kind of net curtain) can reduce fuel bills by as much as 30 per cent and, once put up, can be left in position all year round as it will also shade the plants in summer.

Lining the greenhouse with polythene sheeting is very practical and quickly carried out, and fuel bills can be reduced by up to 40 per cent. Try to use polythene treated by the makers with an ultra-violet inhibitor for longer life as it allows plenty of light to enter the greenhouse during the short winter days. The plastic sheeting is attached to the inside of the greenhouse, ideally leaving an air-gap of about 1–2in (2·5–5cm) between the plastic and the glass. This trapped layer of air forms the actual insulation, not the plastic, so make sure that all the edges overlap to prevent insulating air from escaping. To make really sure, you could smear the plastic edges with a little glycerine to help bond them together.

'Bubble' polythene, in its many forms, is a double-skinned UVI polythene with sealed pockets of air. Its light transmission is not quite so good as that of the single-sheet plastic material, but it is more effective in preventing heat loss. It is fairly expensive, but still worthwhile.

All these plastic materials can easily be fixed to a wooden-framed greenhouse, using drawing-pins or a staple gun. For an aluminium alloy greenhouse you will need to buy special clips. Or you can use a magnetic tape (one strip is stuck to the dry aluminium frame, the other to the plastic sheet).

Vents, of course, need to be lined separately to allow them to operate on spring days when temperatures can rise quite sharply even though the nights are still cool. Also, if you are using a paraffin or gas heater, you will need to ventilate the greenhouse frequently.

During winter, when the evenings are really cold, throw an old carpet or a couple of blankets over the roof to conserve the heat, but do not forget to remove them in the morning.

Unless it is still exceptionally cool, the insulating material can be removed during early spring as seedlings and plants will by then need all the light they can get.

'Bubble' polythene fixed with plastic plugs *Polythene lining fixed with magnetic tape*

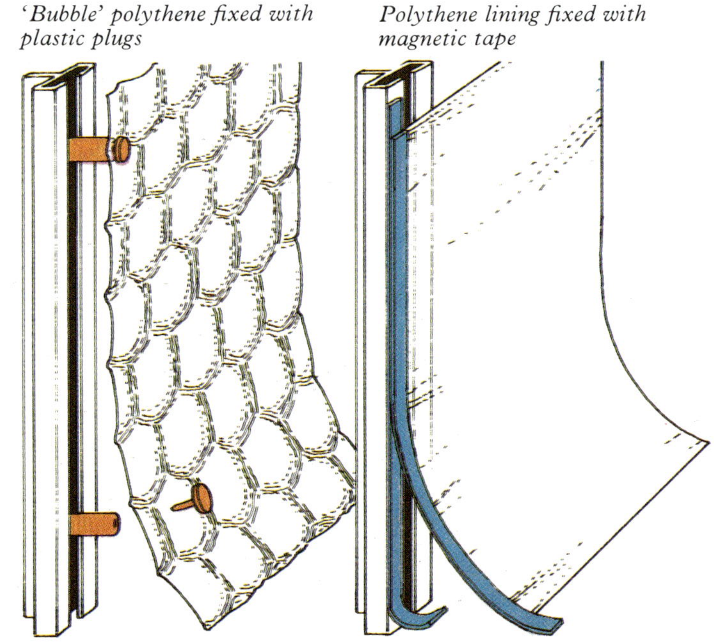

Plants need air – ventilation

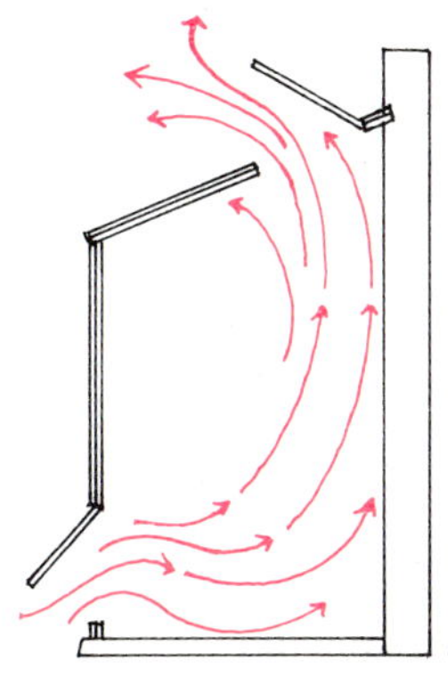

Left: *ventilation is particularly critical in a lean-to. Ensure that air can circulate via low and high-level vents.*

Right: *forced ventilation in a plastic tunnel house.*

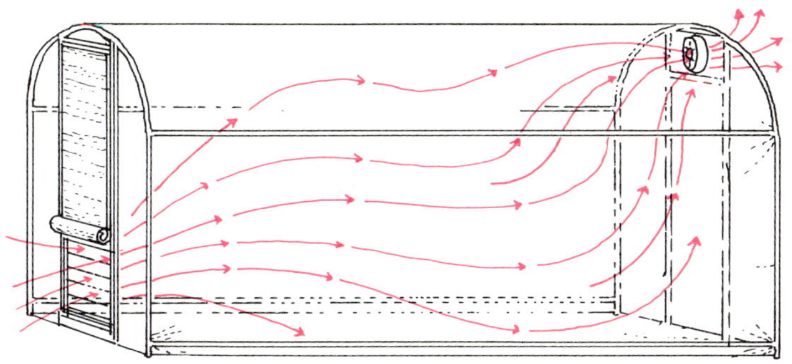

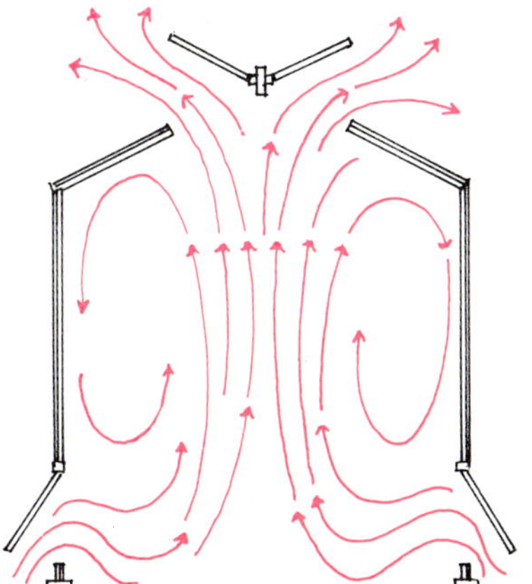

Roof and wall vents allow natural ventilation in summer.

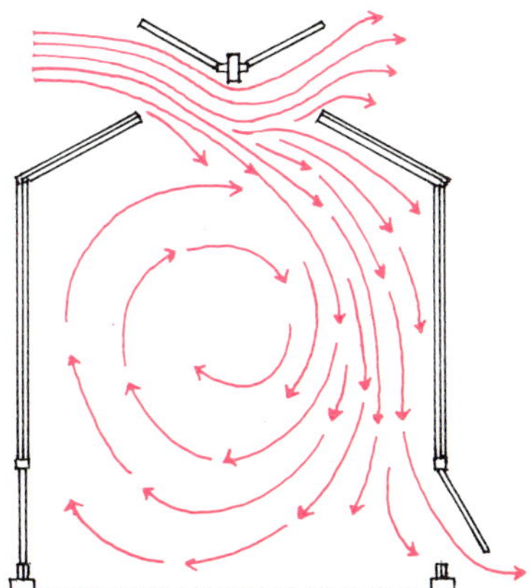

Prevailing winds help to draw out stale, interior air.

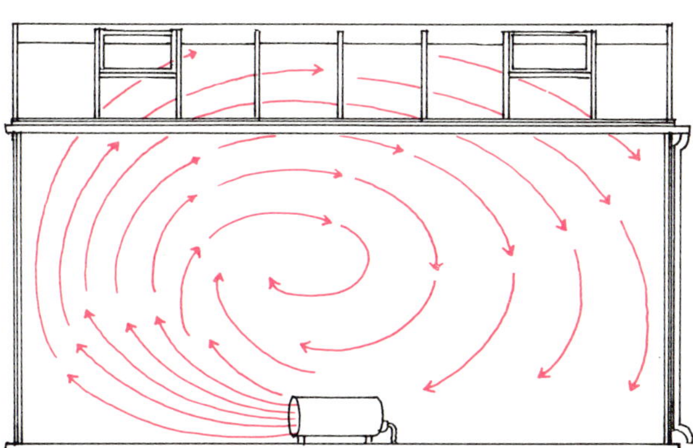

In winter, a fan heater circulates warm air in a closed greenhouse.

Having probably spent money on equipment to heat the greenhouse, paradoxically you should now consider ventilation.

During winter, heat should be retained as much as possible but lack of ventilation can lead to high humidity. Combined with low temperatures this can result in problems with bud drop, or diseases such as botrytis (grey mould) and mildew.

In summer the situation is reversed and you will want to provide high humidity while having the ventilators open to reduce the temperature.

VENTILATION

To provide an effective circulation of air in the greenhouse, there should be one high outlet (ridge vent) and one low-level inlet (or side vent) for every 6ft (2m) length.

When buying a small greenhouse, choose a type that has a ridge vent on either side of the apex, so that you can open the one away from the windward side. This will help to maintain a more steady temperature and avoid damaging draughts.

If side vents are not fitted as standard, it is worth buying one – preferably two – to improve the air flow. If you position one on either side you can use the one away from the prevailing wind. These vents can be of the conventional latched type, sliding or louvred – but whichever type is chosen, it should fit snugly when closed so that there are no cold draughts in winter.

The side vents should be fitted as low as possible; stale warm air rises to the top of the greenhouse where it escapes through the ridge vents, whilst cool fresh air enters through the low side vents, speeding up the whole process of air interchange.

Some of the larger and more expensive greenhouses have a ridge capping that can be raised or lowered mechanically by means of hand-controlled levers or cables, or by automatic vent-openers.

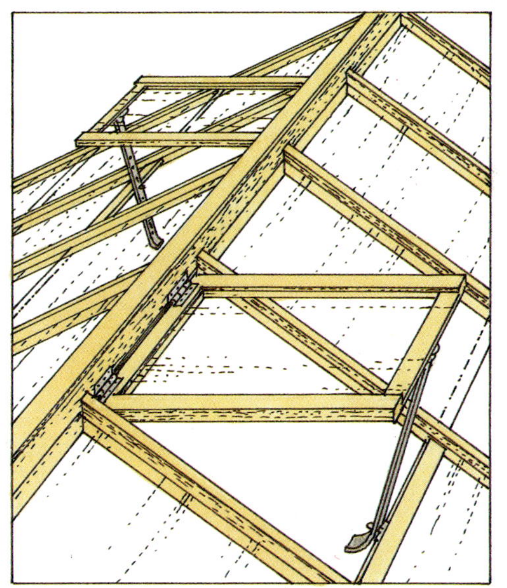

conventional roof ventilators

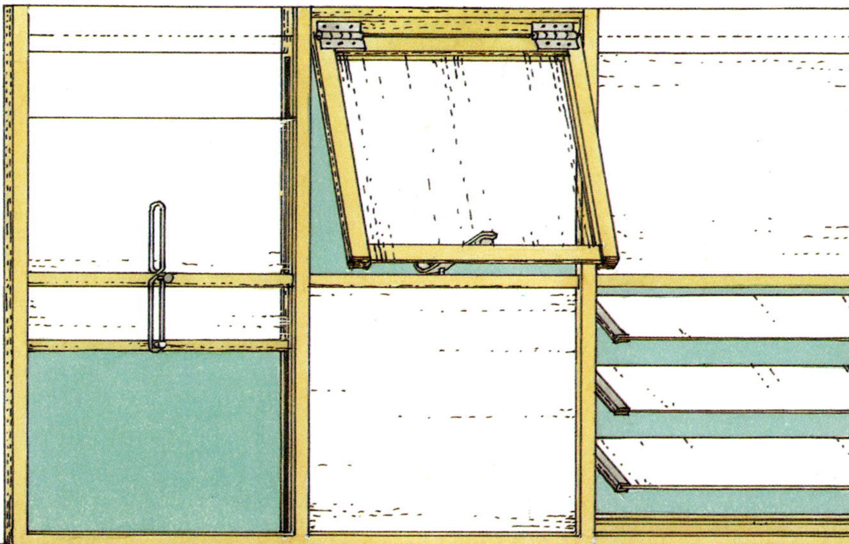

slide ventilator *conventional wall ventilator* *louvre ventilator*

For the gardener who may be out all day and therefore has to leave his greenhouse to the mercies of winds and weather – particularly to fluctuating temperatures – the automatic ventilating arm is a real blessing. There are various makes that can be attached to ridge or louvred vents. They can also operate 'lights' (tops) on some garden frames.

The arm consists of a metal cylinder that is filled with a heat-sensitive compound, usually a kind of wax. When heated, this expands and pushes a piston up the arm. As the compound cools, the piston retracts, so lowering the arm, and the vent slowly closes.

Most types can be adjusted to open at various temperatures and should be attached to the vents away from prevailing winds. Remember to close them down completely during the winter otherwise valuable warmth may be lost.

FANS

A further step towards a controlled environment is the installation of a low-speed electric extractor fan, able to move a large volume of air. The fan should be fitted inside the greenhouse away from the door, high up on the gable end. It should be covered on the outside, by a flush-fitting louvre or flaps which open under pressure, but fall back into the shut position when the fan is switched off. If fitted with a thermostat, it can be pre-set to operate at a certain temperature.

An extractor fan is particularly useful for the plastic greenhouse in which a greater proportion of stagnant air and water vapour is created with a consequent high level of humidity.

As an alternative, a small internal fan can be used to circulate the air in the greenhouse and is often employed all the year round. In winter it reduces the problem of mildew and botrytis (grey mould), and if set high up on the ridge, pointing downwards at an angle of about 10 degrees, it will drive down the warm air that rises, so reducing fuel bills. During hot, still days in summer the constant movement of air will help to lower the temperature.

A fan heater (page 25) can be used to blow cool air around the greenhouse in summer, and can be run thermostatically for economy.

High-speed domestic fans that are used in bathrooms or kitchens are not suitable for use in the greenhouse because they may create artificial draughts, which cause plants to transpire too rapidly.

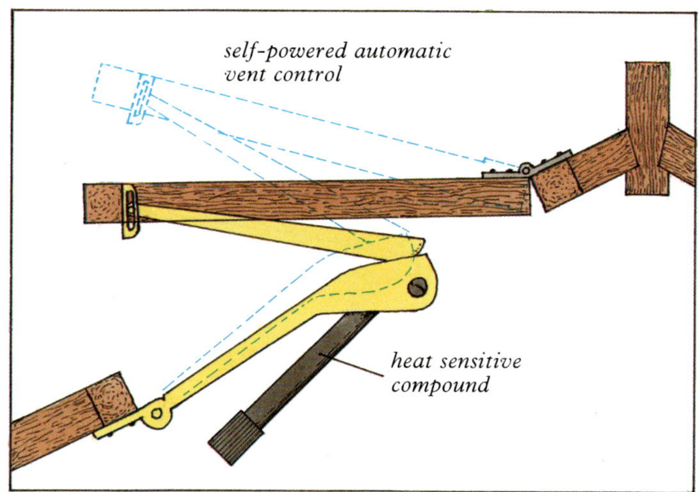

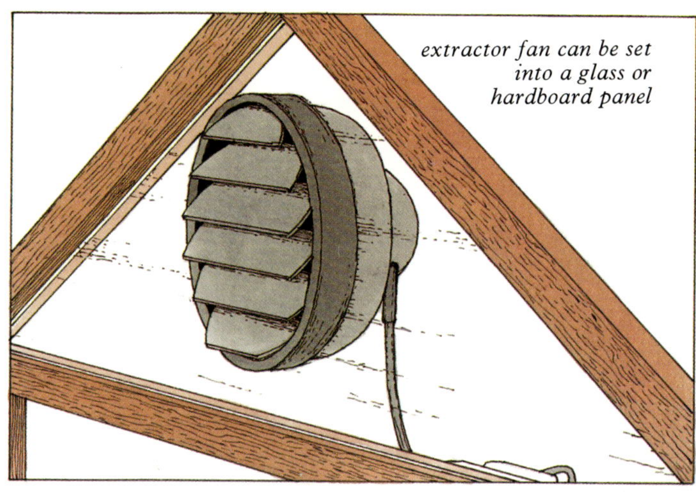

SHADING

During the winter months, every effort is made to let in the maximum amount of light. But, during spring and summer, ways have to be found to restrict solar radiation, so some form of shading must be considered.

The intensity of light can be reduced by the use of blinds, netting, shading washes, plastic sheeting, or strips of muslin.

Blinds made of slatted wood or bamboo should be fitted to the exterior ridge of the greenhouse or plastic Venetian blinds to the interior. The exterior blinds will check direct sun-rays, while at the same time admitting diffused overall daylight to the greenhouse. It is an obvious precaution to anchor them as a protection against high winds.

Exterior blinds can be used in winter as an additional form of frost protection at night.

Plastic roller blinds, usually green-coloured, are easily fitted to the interior of the greenhouse, but it has been found that the colour green absorbs light of wavelengths required by the plants, so it would be better to use opaque plastic. If the blinds are fitted to rails a few inches short of the ridge, it will allow the air to circulate and the heat absorbed by the blinds to dissipate.

You can use a lime-wash or well diluted emulsion paint, but it is much better to use an 'electrostatic' shading wash. This is a liquid concentrate which is diluted with water and painted or sprayed on, in varying degrees of density. Because of its electro-

exterior blinds

shading paint

interior blinds

static quality, it will stay in position even during heavy rain spells, but only needs a quick rub with a dry duster to remove it. A wood-framed greenhouse should preferably be painted rather than sprayed as it would be difficult to avoid splattering paint on to the wood and spoiling its appearance.

There is another form of paint-on shading that is opaque and white when dry but becomes translucent when wet, allowing more light to enter the greenhouse on rainy days.

If you are unable to reach up to the ridge, lash a wide paintbrush to the end of a long handle, or use a soft broom. To remove the wash, just cover the broom with a dry duster, working it back and forth until the glass is clean.

THERMOMETERS

Every greenhouse should have an accurate thermometer – preferably the minimum/maximum type as these record both the lowest point during the night and the highest point reached during the day. This information is valuable as it offers solid facts on which to base heating, ventilating and shading requirements.

All thermometers should be positioned out of direct sunlight and where there is good air circulation.

You can buy a thermometer that sounds an alarm when the temperature is dropping towards freezing.

THERMOSTATS

A thermostat coupled to a heating element will automatically maintain the desired temperature, and will save money by ensuring that current is only used when necessary. Thermostats are usually bi-metallic (they are made of two strips of different metals that expand or contract at varying rates whenever the temperature changes), activating a switch that turns on the heat source.

Most thermostats have a dial which can be pre-set to a desired temperature. It is wise to check this occasionally against an accurate thermometer, and adjust the setting if necessary.

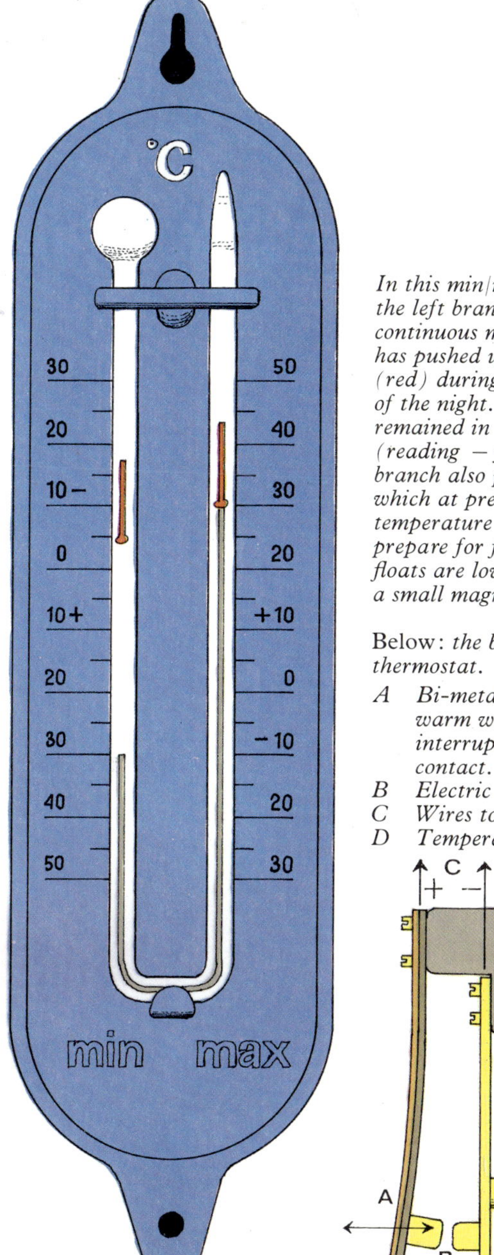

In this min/max thermometer, the left branch of the continuous mercury column has pushed up a tiny float (red) during the coldest hour of the night. The float has remained in that position (reading −5°C). The right branch also pushes up a float which at present shows a temperature of +30°C. To prepare for fresh readings, the floats are lowered by means of a small magnet.

Below: *the basic elements of a thermostat.*

A *Bi-metallic strip bends in warm weather and so interrupts the electronic contact.*
B *Electric contacts*
C *Wires to heater*
D *Temperature setting knob*

Plants need water

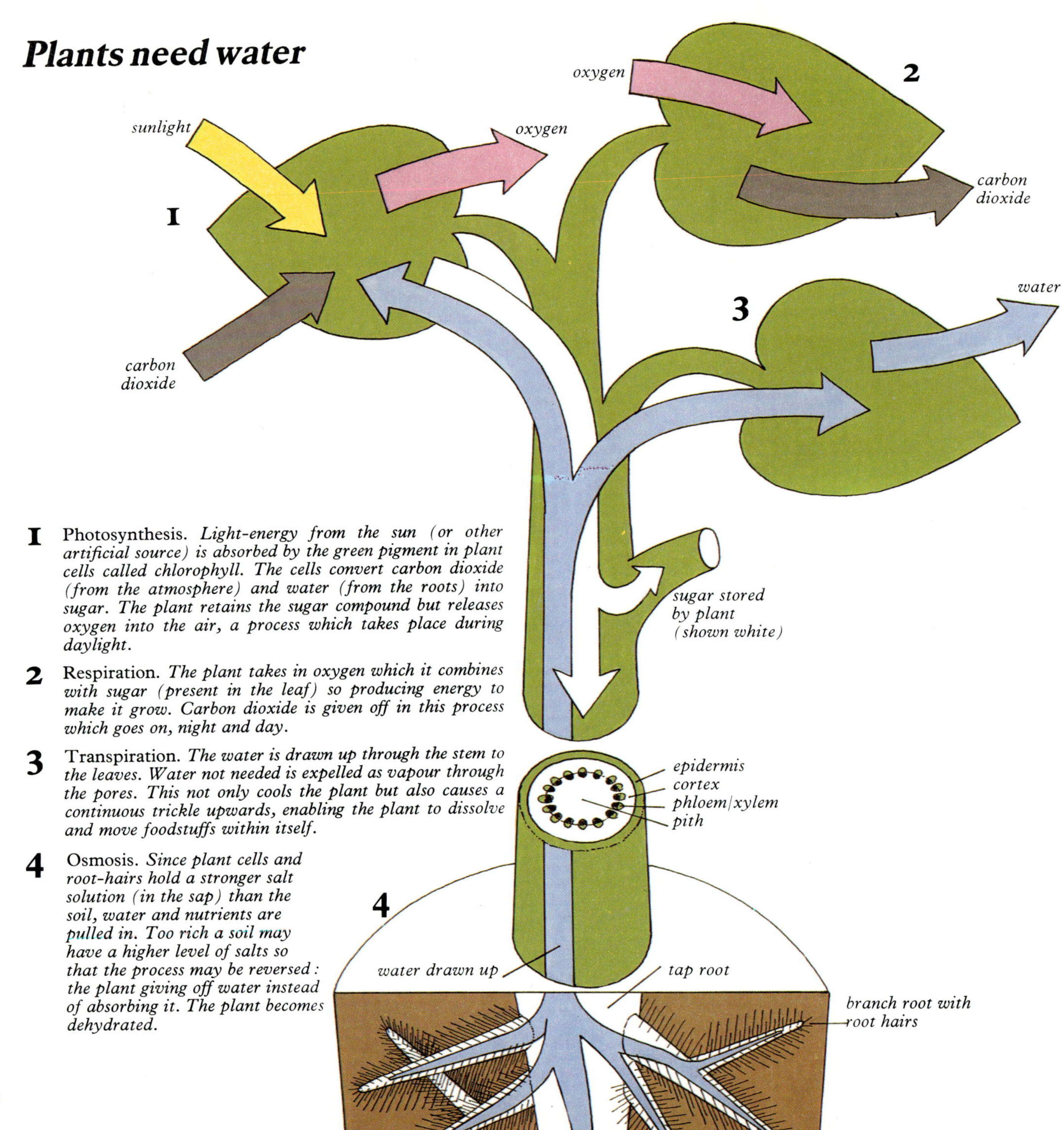

I Photosynthesis. *Light-energy from the sun (or other artificial source) is absorbed by the green pigment in plant cells called chlorophyll. The cells convert carbon dioxide (from the atmosphere) and water (from the roots) into sugar. The plant retains the sugar compound but releases oxygen into the air, a process which takes place during daylight.*

2 Respiration. *The plant takes in oxygen which it combines with sugar (present in the leaf) so producing energy to make it grow. Carbon dioxide is given off in this process which goes on, night and day.*

3 Transpiration. *The water is drawn up through the stem to the leaves. Water not needed is expelled as vapour through the pores. This not only cools the plant but also causes a continuous trickle upwards, enabling the plant to dissolve and move foodstuffs within itself.*

4 Osmosis. *Since plant cells and root-hairs hold a stronger salt solution (in the sap) than the soil, water and nutrients are pulled in. Too rich a soil may have a higher level of salts so that the process may be reversed: the plant giving off water instead of absorbing it. The plant becomes dehydrated.*

Plants extract water from compost through their roots. Besides carrying nutrients with it, water keeps plants turgid so that they grow strong and healthy. Pot plants should never be waterlogged, however. In winter, most are often dormant or resting and will only need a little water, or even none at all.

Overwatering can cause root rot, bud, flower or foliage drop, yellowing leaves, and wilting. Should you notice that the soil is sticky and has an unpleasant smell, take the plant out of its pot, remove as much of the compost as possible, pot it up with new compost . . . and pray.

WHEN TO WATER

There is no hard-and-fast rule for watering individual plants – it is mostly a matter of experience gradually gained over at least a season. All too often, plants are killed by kindness – they are overwatered when the compost is in fact quite moist, even though the surface may look dry.

To check that a plant needs watering, weigh the pot in your hand – if it feels quite heavy, it is moist enough; if it is light in weight, it may be dry. But bear in mind that clay pots are heavier than plastic ones. The surface soil may look dry, but if you remove a bit of it, you will probably find that the soil underneath is, in fact, quite moist.

After some time you will be able to check the state of the compost by touch and sight. To be really certain, you could use a moisture meter which gives a more accurate answer.

A moisture meter is another device that will give the earnest gardener real facts about the condition of the compost, and therefore the state of his plants. There are many types of meter on the market, most of them having a long probe which is thrust into the compost or soil. The moisture content of the compost can then be read by means of a moving needle, a light, or by the rapidity of a series of clicks.

In summer, particularly on hot days, all plants need frequent attention. Photosynthesis will be rapid, and so will be the water-loss, which can cause serious wilting. A tomato plant may need a couple of gallons (perhaps 10 litres) of water on a really hot day.

It is better to soak a container thoroughly, but not so that water pours out of the bottom as a lot of valuable nutrients will be lost. The surface of compost in a pot should never be flush with the rim, otherwise water will flood the staging rather than seeping down to the roots.

The roof surface of a greenhouse represents a large area that can be used to collect precious rainwater, if you use a water-butt. A tightly fitting lid will keep out leaves and debris that would otherwise contaminate the water. Because static water easily harbours fungi spores and bacteria, which may adversely affect the plants, mains water is healthier for the majority of plants. Try to use rainwater, however, for those kinds that are sensitive to lime.

A simple but most valuable aid for the greenhouse is a well designed watering-can. The beginner may be confused by the many sizes and shapes available, as well as being undecided as to the merits of galvanised, enamelled metal, and light-weight plastic watering-cans. The most useful shape is one that has a long spout which can reach through a cluster of pot plants to the back of the staging, and a curved spout-end attachment will ensure that water does not splash other plants. A fine 'rose' is essential when watering delicate seedlings or for damping down the central path of a greenhouse during hot summer weather.

A small plastic can with a long, thin, curved spout will be needed if you have plants growing on high shelves or in hanging-baskets. A large can is difficult to lift.

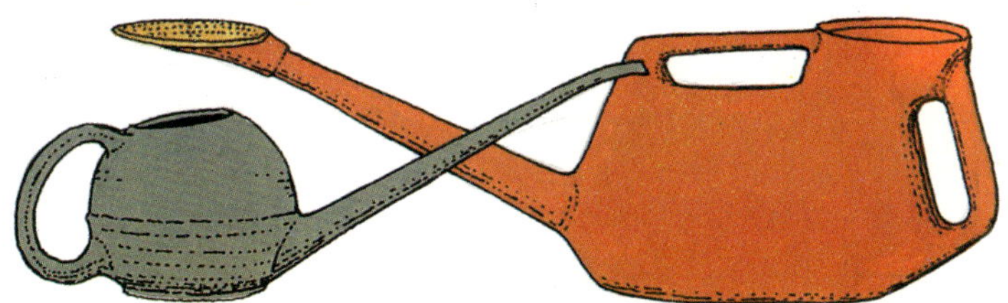

CAPILLARY MATTING

Watering plants by hand can be a fairly arduous task if there are many of them, and during a hot summer can turn into a real headache if you are away during the day. The need to find someone else who will do the job twice a day also dampens the desire to go on holiday for any length of time!

A cheap and simple way to reduce this problem is to install capillary matting. It is lightweight, convenient to use, absorbent, and can be tailored to fit any staging. With care, the matting should last for two to three years.

First check that the staging is absolutely level before covering it with a sheet of rigid plastic or a thin metal sheet if the staging has wide-spaced slats, or plastic-covered wire mesh or rods.

Capillary mats can be kept moist by hand, but it is more useful to arrange an automatic feed. If you have wooden staging, cut a length of guttering, blocking off the ends, and fix it to the front of the staging to act as a water reservoir. Then cover the surface with a piece of black heavy-gauge polythene and place the capillary matting on top of that. It can be trimmed with a pair of scissors, but make sure it laps into the gutter.

For aluminium staging, repeat the above process except for the guttering. Instead, stand a washing-up bowl at one end of the staging, place a couple of wicks in it with their other ends resting on the matting so that capillary action draws water out of the bowl and is absorbed by the matting. Alternatively, turn a large bottle upside down in a bowl of water with its neck just below the water level, with a wick leading to the matting (see below). Both arrangements need a daily topping up.

If you have large trays, you can line them with capillary matting, making sure that a wick connects each one. Water can then be supplied by means of a drip nozzle from a plastic tank that holds about 4 gallons (18 litres).

A weak solution of nutrients can be introduced into any of the watering systems.

Black, green, or white capillary matting will, in time, become clogged with compost, roots and algae. This can be cleared to some extent by turning the matting over, by washing it gently in warm soapy water, or by leaving it to soak for about an hour in a weak solution of bleach (which has to be thoroughly rinsed out afterwards).

Below: *various watering systems using capillary matting.*

Plastic pots are better than clay ones because they do not become covered in algae so easily. For use on capillary matting, neither type of pot should be crocked, and the compost should be damp before the pot is pressed onto the matting. Clay pots may need to have a wick pressed into the compost through the hole in the base for effective capillary action. Use a commercially made wick or insert a strip of spare capillary matting.

Capillary matting not only feeds water to the plants, but the water given off its surface will evaporate into the greenhouse area generally, so creating a welcome degree of humidity during warm weather. On the other hand, you may find there is too much moisture and humidity in winter, so the matting should not be employed for a while.

TRICKLE IRRIGATION

Trickle systems are excellent for irrigating pot plants, seed trays, and borders. They can be operated automatically or manually.

There are several types on the market. The 'spaghetti' system, which is the simplest, comprises a large diameter tube with a series of very narrow tubes leading off it at intervals. At the end of each narrow tube there is an adjustable nozzle to control the rate of drip to suit the plant's particular needs. Many types of trickle system can be bought ready-made, but whichever system you employ, check the output from time to time to make sure your plants are receiving the correct amount of water.

It is not such a precise method of watering as capillary matting, but is still a boon for the busy gardener.

SPRINKLER LINES

In this system, water is supplied to the plants in the form of an overhead mist covering the growing area, increasing humidity in the greenhouse at the same time. The 'spray-line', which is suspended overhead, is usually either a rigid alloy or flexible plastic tube (which may need additional support to stop it sagging). The action is controlled manually, or electrically by means of a special detector – a moisture-sensitive pad, or an 'electronic leaf' detector (see page 38).

One of the main drawbacks of this system, is that when growth is lush, the water-spray will not easily be able to penetrate through the foliage to reach the pots. But for border plants such as tomatoes and lettuces it is quite useful.

Finding the most practical equipment for your needs

STAGING

There is such a wide range of staging on offer that it is virtually impossible not to find a type to suit your needs exactly. Staging tops usually come in widths of 18in (45cm), 24in (60cm) and 30in (75cm), either of wood or aluminium. Of course, many D-I-Y gardeners may want to build their own staging of wood, brick or concrete.

If you buy ready-made staging, make sure it can take the weight of your plants. Cross-bracing will add strength for heavy pots, seed trays and possibly even growing bags.

So that air can circulate freely, staging should be placed in such a way that there is a gap of a few inches between it and the glass of the greenhouse wall.

If your staging consists of two or three tiers, it is a good idea to cover all but the bottom tier with a sheet of plastic so that water and debris cannot fall onto the plants underneath.

Slatted and wire-mesh staging allow free circulation of air in the winter and are therefore particularly suitable for cold or cool greenhouses. In summer, metal or plastic trays can be laid on the wire mesh surface and filled with gravel, or lined with capillary matting.

Wood staging is usually made from treated western red cedar, or in some cases from marine-ply slats. The units are free-standing and their legs should rest on bricks so that they do not come into contact with the soil. They are usually slatted and can be bought as single, double or triple tiers.

The constantly damp environment of most greenhouses will eventually be harmful to any wood. It must therefore be cleaned thoroughly each season and coated with linseed oil or with a preservative recommended by the manufacturer.

Aluminium staging can be slatted, fitted with trays, or made of plastic-coated wire-mesh. It is easy to assemble, lightweight, maintenance-free and waterproof, and can be arranged in single or double tiers.

Brick or concrete benching

Unlike the ready-made staging units which, like furniture, can be moved around or attached to the greenhouse wall in different places, brick and concrete benching is more or less permanent and therefore needs to be planned carefully. Because this type of staging is heavy, it should be erected on a firm base, particularly if constructed on sandy or clay ground.

If well executed, laid brick or cast concrete benching will have a long life and will stand up well to trickle irrigation and overhead spray watering. Brick in particular provides the greenhouse gardener with an extra bonus: as the sun shines on a brick wall, heat is absorbed by it, and retained. At night, warmth from the bricks is gradually released, so keeping the temperature in the greenhouse a few degrees higher than would otherwise be the case. Concrete, on the other hand, is not so good at retaining heat.

SHELVES

Apart from staging or benching, shelves offer useful extra growing space, particularly at a time when the greenhouse is bursting at the seams with seedlings and plants. They are also a practical way to display a host of trailing plants.

Shelves need to be robust, and those made of wood or metal can easily be fixed to the sides of a greenhouse or, if there is enough headroom, just under the ridge. Try to avoid positioning them where they cast shadows onto plants placed under them. As the plants grow bigger, shelves can, of course, be removed to make space. Or they can be put up in other places to adjust to different light conditions.

Shelves can be kept clean by lining them with a sheet of plastic to catch water drips and debris.

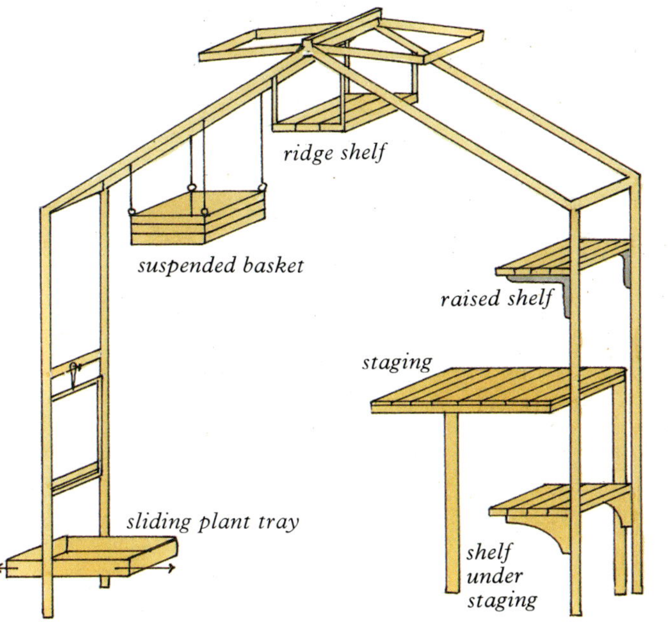

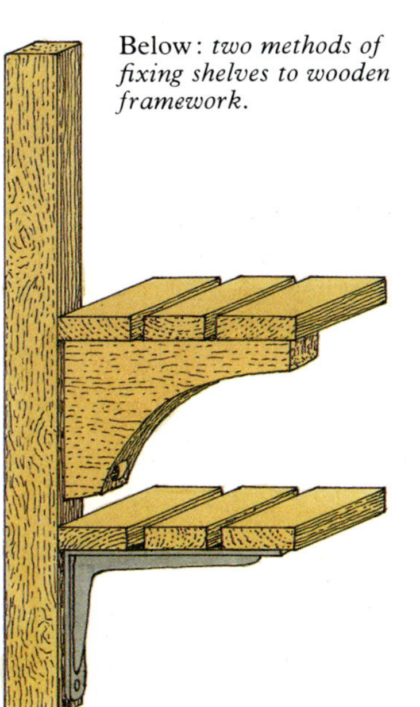

Below: *two methods of fixing shelves to wooden framework.*

Tray-shelf attached to a slotted aluminium glazing bar.

SUPPLEMENTARY LIGHTING

The winter sun may have only a fraction of the intensity of the summer sun. In addition, its duration in higher latitudes may only be half that of a summer's day. To make full use of the greenhouse – to make summers seem longer, in fact – you can install a strip light which will enable you to work during the evenings. It should be positioned so that it casts a minimum amount of shadow over the working area.

To stimulate plant growth, and to extend 'day length', you can install special fluorescent tubes suitable for plant growth (if you find them difficult to buy, try an aquarium shop). Mercury vapour lamps can also be bought. Both kinds should be positioned close to the plants. It is advisable to ask the supplier for exact details about the effective output of the lights, and where to place them.

CONTROLS FOR ELECTRICAL AIDS

Some mist propagation units and sprinkler lines are controlled by an electro-mechanical balance detector, which is a foam pad attached to the end of a balance arm. The pad gradually absorbs moisture when the area is being sprayed, and when quite wet will tip the arm, causing a switch to break contact and cut off the spray. As moisture evaporates from the cuttings and the foam pad lightens, the arm rises to activate further misting or sprinkling. The foam pad can be moved along its mounting arm to control the frequency of watering.

'Electronic leaf' detectors are used for some mist units. The 'leaves' are terminals; as moisture evaporates from the cuttings, the terminals dry and break an electrical circuit which is a signal for the mist to be switched on. As the terminals become damp, the water is switched off.

Solar control detectors are sometimes used for capillary, trickle, and sprinkler line watering systems, and occasionally for mist units. They are governed by light intensity; a photo-electric cell absorbs light which, when it reaches a pre-determined level, will activate the system. The sunnier the weather, the more often the system operates. At night, when the system would not normally operate, a simple override control can be used.

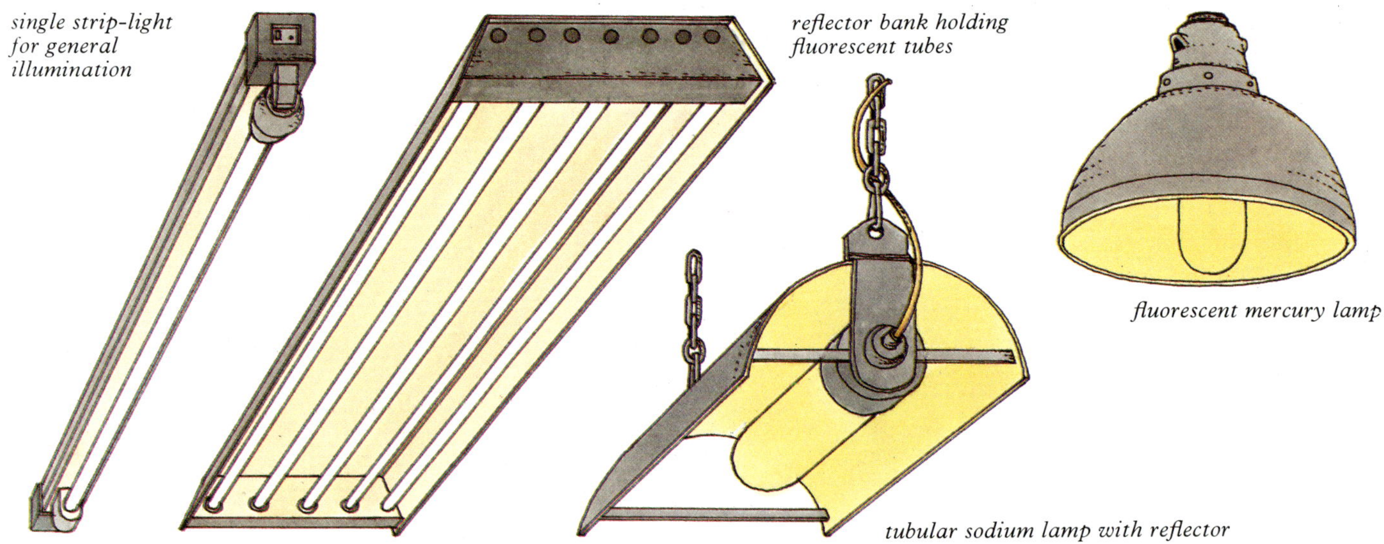

single strip-light for general illumination

reflector bank holding fluorescent tubes

fluorescent mercury lamp

tubular sodium lamp with reflector

PROPAGATORS

To heat the whole greenhouse to a temperature suitable for germinating seeds and rooting cuttings would be very expensive, but a propagator enables you to heat a small space economically.

For the beginner with an unheated greenhouse that has no electricity laid on, there are plastic seed trays with transparent lids. They are cheap to buy and can always be placed on a windowledge indoors, and with care should last for a few seasons. Although unheated they do provide some warmth and protection.

Commercially made propagators simply have a dome over an ordinary seed tray. Note the ventilators on top. The sloping sides allow condensation to run down the sides, so avoiding harmful dripping onto seedlings.

Right: *ready-made plastic dome and pot unit. It is made in many sizes.*

Far right: *a small pot-propagator can be made at home with some wire and a polythene bag.*

Seeds can be bought ready sown in vermiculite in their own plastic propagator. Simply remove and invert the lid, add water and keep the tray in a warm place.

An ordinary seed tray can also serve as a propagator base. When you have sown the seeds, make a dome out of wire and polythene sheeting.

Right: *a paraffin-heated propagator. It heats water held in the bottom tank.*

Below: *one of the smallest propagators. It consists of a double-insulated heating panel which supports a seed tray. It uses 16 Watts at 230/250 volt A.C.*

Below: *electrically heated propagator with thermostat costs about 12 pence per week to run. (50 Watts at 230/250 volts A.C.)*

Alternatively, there are paraffin-heated propagators, which use a small burner to heat a flat water-filled tank on which you can stand seed trays or pots.

If there is a convenient electricity supply, the range of units increases quite dramatically. If you just want to experiment, or only want to raise a few seeds at a time, it is possible to buy a small double-insulated panel. It is large enough to take a standard-sized seed tray and can be used in the greenhouse or placed on a windowledge. It should, however, not be used in an unheated cold greenhouse in winter, as the demand for raising a very low night temperature to that required for propagation could be too great for the heating element to cope with.

There are rather bigger, more expensive, bases that have built-in thermostatically controlled elements. The base should be covered with a layer of damp sand before seed trays, pots or cuttings are placed in it. The covering can either be a polythene sheet fitted over a galvanised wire frame, or individual rigid plastic covers that fit standard-sized seed trays.

Most heated propagators come complete with a transparent plastic top, usually with some means of adjusting ventilation.

PROPAGATING BENCHES

It is cheaper to construct a progating bench than to buy a ready-made unit if you want to propagate a number of cuttings.

Staging with slats or wire-mesh must be covered with thick polythene sheeting, roofing felt, or a sheet of expanded polystyrene sheeting. The whole area can then be surrounded by four treated wooden boards 9–10in (23–25cm) deep, with the corners joined securely. To avoid rusting, use galvanised or stainless-steel clips, nuts and bolts, or screws.

Spread 2in (5cm) of coarse washed river sand over the base and level it before laying the soil-warming cable (see page 48). As a guide to the amount of cable needed to provide sufficient bottom heat, you will need a 75W cable for $7\frac{1}{2}$sq ft (0·7sq m), a 150W cable for 15sq ft (1·4sq m) and a 300W cable for 30sq ft (2·8sq m). Cover the cables with a further 2–3in (5–7·5cm) of sand and moisten it to ensure an even distribution of warmth.

It is a good idea to cover the top with a pane of glass or a sheet of rigid plastic to raise the temperature and humidity still further.

Additional cables can be clipped to the inside of the case to warm the air – a 75W cable for up to 5sq ft (0·5sq m), a 150W cable for up to 10sq ft (1sq m) and a 300W cable for up to 20sq ft (1·8sq m).

Ideally, the propagating bench should be run thermostatically for economy of fuel, and the interior painted white to intensify light and to promote rapid, sturdy growth. To keep the temperatures more even, the space around seed trays and pots can be packed with damp peat or vermiculite.

Cuttings will root better and more quickly under automatically controlled mist spraying. Misting prevents wilting and young soft growth is encouraged to root more rapidly. If misting is going to be used, the base should be made of expanded polystyrene, and drilled with holes at regular intervals to ensure good drainage. It will also prevent the rooting medium from becoming waterlogged.

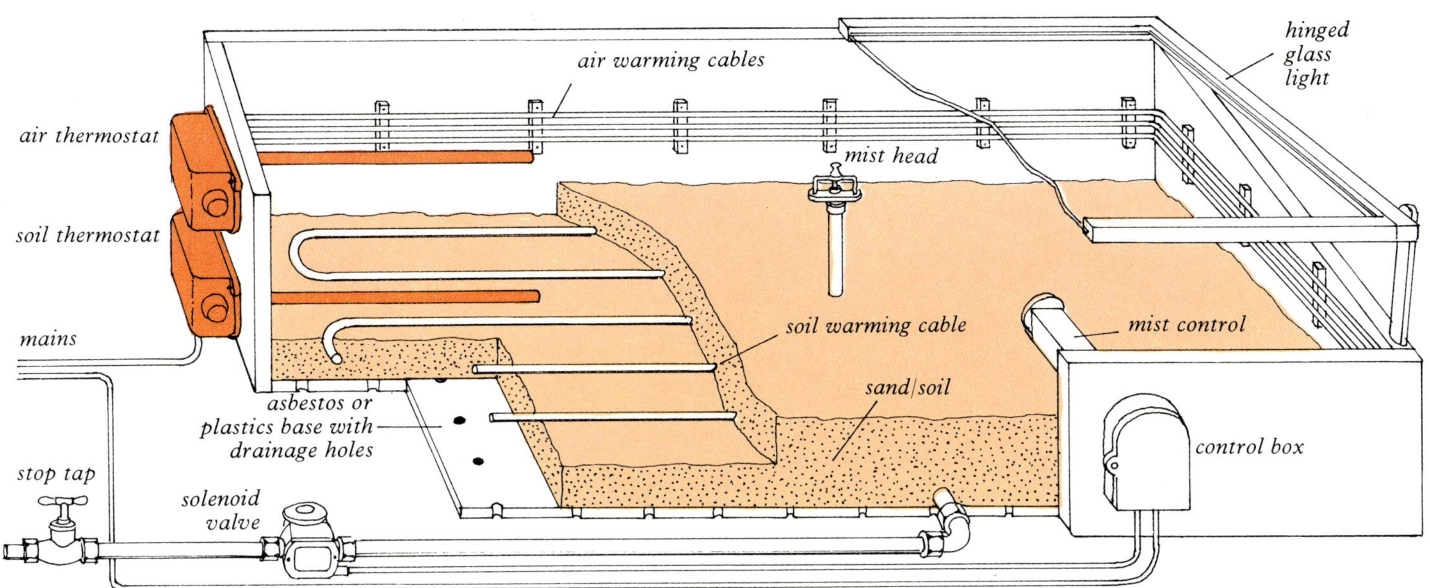

Looking after your greenhouse

Regular maintenance of a greenhouse or garden frame, and the equipment, is essential. It makes sense to carry this out in the autumn before the greenhouse or frame is stocked with plants for overwintering.

TREATING TIMBER

Autumn is the best time to treat a wood-framed greenhouse as the wood will be dry. It will then absorb linseed oil or preservative far more rapidly.

You should only need to treat the timber every two or three years, but if the wood is not cared for it will gradually turn grey from bleaching by the sun and the oils will dry out completely.

Use a wire brush to clean the wood before using a clean paintbrush or rag to work linseed oil into the grain (boiled linseed oil dries more rapidly than raw). Alternatively you can use a proprietary cedar preservative to give it a nice reddish-brown colour. Never paint the wood with creosote unless the greenhouse can be left empty for many months.

If the greenhouse is to be painted, the bare wood must be perfectly dry before work commences.

ALUMINIUM GREENHOUSES

Aluminium greenhouses can be left without maintenance for long periods. The metal will gradually dull as a protective film of whitish oxide forms, but this is harmless. If you find it objectionable you can clean the metal with household wire-wool, or even rub it down with a little wax polish.

CLEANING GLASS

Dirty glass will radiate precious heat away from the greenhouse as well as reducing the light intensity so it really pays to clean it well both inside and outside. You can use a water softener to help.

Overlapped panes of glass soon become caked with algae and look unsightly. A thin strip of metal or a plastic plant label can be inserted gently between the panes to remove some of the growth, but if it will not budge use a solution of kettle descaler or a bath stain remover diluted with a little washing-up liquid. Try using a medicine dropper to apply the liquid. The solution should be left for a few hours before squirting water from a hose through the overlaps, from the inside of the greenhouse so that it is washed through to the outside.

If you have been using a mist propagator during the summer and there is a build-up of lime on the glass, the same solutions can be used to clean it.

Small cracks in panes of glass can be repaired with wide strips of glazing tape, which can also be used to repair torn and split plastic material. If a whole pane of glass has to be replaced, it is a good idea to take a piece of it with you as a guide to thickness when ordering a replacement.

CLEANING STAGING

Slatted wood staging should be scrubbed down thoroughly with a suitable disinfectant (a garden shop or garden centre will be able to recommend one, but follow the instructions carefully). Rinse with clean water. It is best to do this outside the greenhouse. As it is quite a smelly job, wear rubber gloves.

Aluminium staging will probably only need to be cleaned with warm water and washing-up liquid.

Staging or benching gravel should be cleaned by placing it in a fine sieve and running clean water from a hosepipe over it. If it is encrusted with algae and moss, it is wise to discard it.

Capillary matting should be removed for cleaning (see page 34), and must be really dry before being stored away for the winter.

CHECKING EQUIPMENT

Check that all the electrical and soil-warming equipment is properly earthed and functioning correctly before winter arrives. You may need the advice of a qualified electrician.

Paraffin heaters will probably need thorough cleaning and the wicks may need to be trimmed or replaced with new ones.

Gas cylinders should be checked and new bottles ordered if necessary.

GENERAL HYGIENE

Corners, cracks and holes are potential hiding places for such horrors as red spider mites, earwigs, aphids, slugs, snails, woodlice, and fungus spores. Unless dealt with properly, they will attack plants during the winter months with dire results.

Remove all the plants and scrub down the interior. A weak solution of diluted bleach or a household disinfectant will be more effective than using hot, soapy water. Where there are algae, the area should be well scrubbed with an algicide solution.

Any weeds under the staging should be pulled or dug up. To over come the weed problem, it would be better to put down a 3in (7·5cm) layer of gravel, or even concrete slabs.

All greenhouses will benefit from being fumigated periodically. You can buy greenhouse smokes containing an insecticide or a fungicide – or both.

The best time to fumigate is in the evening when temperatures are not too high and there is no bright sunshine, otherwise the closed-up greenhouse may overheat.

Some of the fumigants look like cone-shaped fireworks, and you light the blue touch-paper at the top. Many gardeners use this form of fumigation regularly throughout the year. When they are ignited, a lot of smoke is produced and you should retreat at once. Always follow the manufacturer's recommendations carefully, and check which plants may be affected so that you can remove them first.

You can also buy an electrically run fumigator that is a permanent fixture in the greenhouse. These are popular with commercial growers; they vaporise various chemicals to treat greenhouse pests and diseases.

Greenhouse borders should be drenched thoroughly with a soil steriliser. All plants must be removed before digging over the border and drenching it with the solution. The bed should then be covered with a thick sheet of polythene to retain the fumes. Follow the manufacturer's instructions carefully, and avoid inhaling any fumes. After about a week you should be able to ventilate the greenhouse for a while to ensure all the fumes have gone, but it is advisable not to grow plants in the border for at least six weeks after application.

Another way to deal with border soil is to replace the loam to a depth of about 2ft (60cm), taking care to avoid spillage as it is removed.

An easier – but probably more costly – answer is to use growing bags.

Long, pillow-shaped growing bags, filled with a peat compost, can be used on borders as temporary beds, and there are smaller ones available which can be placed on staging. They can be used to raise tomatoes, aubergines, courgettes or capsicums (peppers), though you must take care with watering. As the plants and compost are contained in the plastic bag, there is no fear that their roots will be in contact with diseased soil.

Growing bags are best discarded at the end of each season, and the contents spread over garden beds as a form of mulch.

CONTAINERS AND WATER BUTTS

All pots, seed trays, watering-cans and water butts should be scrubbed thoroughly before being stored or re-used. Compost bags should have their tops covered or they should be stored in small bins with tight-fitting lids to avoid contamination.

Garden frames

TYPES OF GARDEN FRAME

A garden frame is useful in its own right, but it is also an ideal adjunct to the greenhouse.

Garden frames have been around for a long time. Records show that the Emperor Caesar Tiberius was advised to eat a cucumber a day, so his gardener was ordered to grow them – luckily his gardener knew his cucumbers! Pits were dug and half-filled with fermenting dung which provided warmth, and the tops were covered with transparent sheets of mica.

You will find that garden frames are invaluable as a half-way house for plants or seedlings that need to be hardened off before being bedded out. They are also useful for housing resting plants that would otherwise take up valuable greenhouse space. As with greenhouses, they can be used for growing out-of-season crops.

A garden frame is, in fact, a small and relatively inexpensive mini greenhouse. It has the advantage of being cheaper to heat. If it is small enough, you can even use it as a propagator for raising plants in a cool greenhouse.

If you are considering buying a frame but suffer from back trouble, it might be possible to raise it to a more comfortable working height to avoid a lot of stooping. This can be done by building a platform of bricks or concrete blocks encompassed by a low wall with the frame set on top of it – or by placing the frame on a really sturdy bench, see page 37.

Not only people but plants too have problems with height, so if you intend to use the frame to protect or harden off pot plants, try to buy one with sufficient head-room. On the other hand, if you only intend raising or hardening off seedlings or just want to

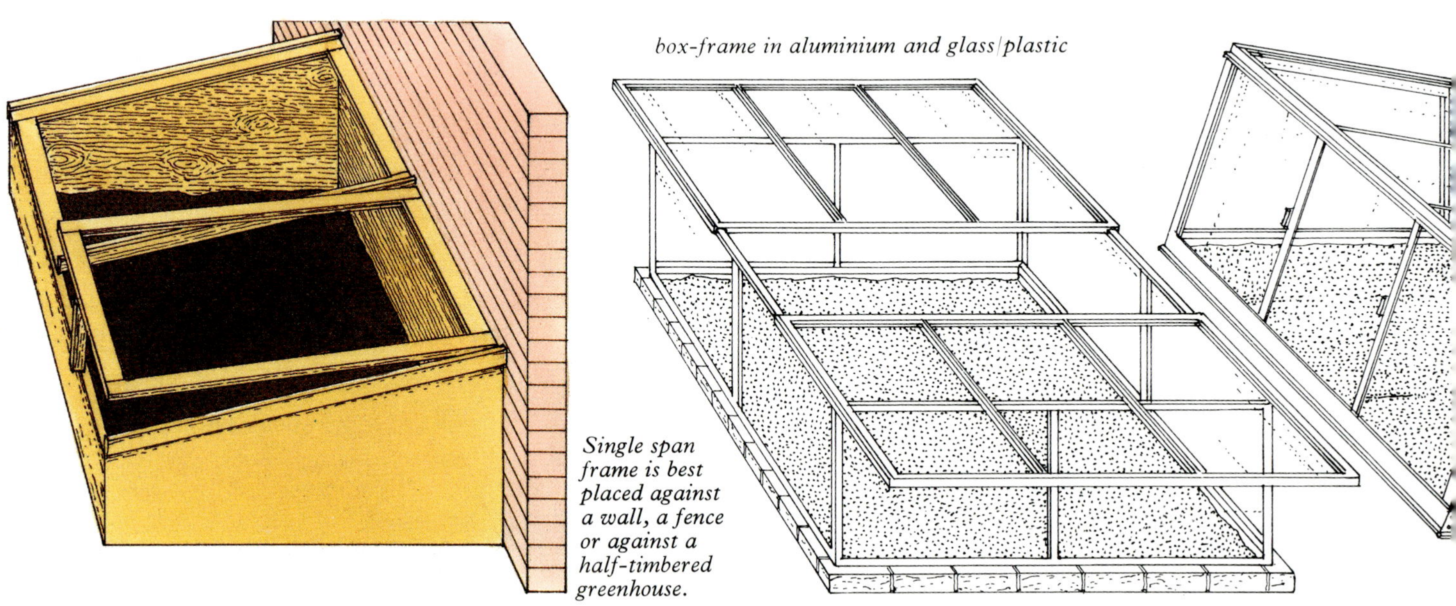

box-frame in aluminium and glass/plastic

Single span frame is best placed against a wall, a fence or against a half-timbered greenhouse.

propagate cuttings, you can obviously manage with less head-room. You will almost certainly find one that gives you ample height more useful in the long run.

Another important factor when buying a frame is the ease with which it can be ventilated. Some plastic ones are supplied with roll-tops. Glass frames usually have a hinged or sliding top – some of the more expensive types have the added bonus of sliding side panes as well. Whichever type you buy, make sure that the panels can either be completely removed and stacked in a safe place, or their tops hinged open as far as possible during hot summer weather. Some frames come complete with casement stays to support the top in the open position – but make sure that they are sturdy. If the frame has no form of prop you can easily make one by cutting a couple of steps into a large piece of seasoned wood. During spring and autumn, when only little air is needed, a thick wedge will provide sufficient ventilation.

Because an early sharp burst of sunlight can scorch the leaves of plants, some shading is useful from late spring onwards. A light application of a shading wash or a close-mesh net thrown over the structure will reduce the sun's intensity.

CHOOSING THE SITE

Unlike greenhouses, which come in many shapes and designs, garden frames have only two basic shapes. The first of these has a single span, with 'lights' (another name for the top) which slope in only one direction. It should be sited east to west so that the 'lights' slope to the south, and is therefore best placed against a wall, fence or abutting a greenhouse. The other shape of garden frame is the double-span with an apex roof like a house; these frames are best sited 'free standing' north to south to take full advantage of the prevailing light.

If the frame is to be used mainly for summer pot plants, the best place for it is a reasonably shady area. For vegetable crops it should be sited in an open, sunny position, and if more than one frame is used they can either be placed back to back or in a row. Do not place a frame in a corner by a wall, or in a dip in the garden that you know to be a frost pocket.

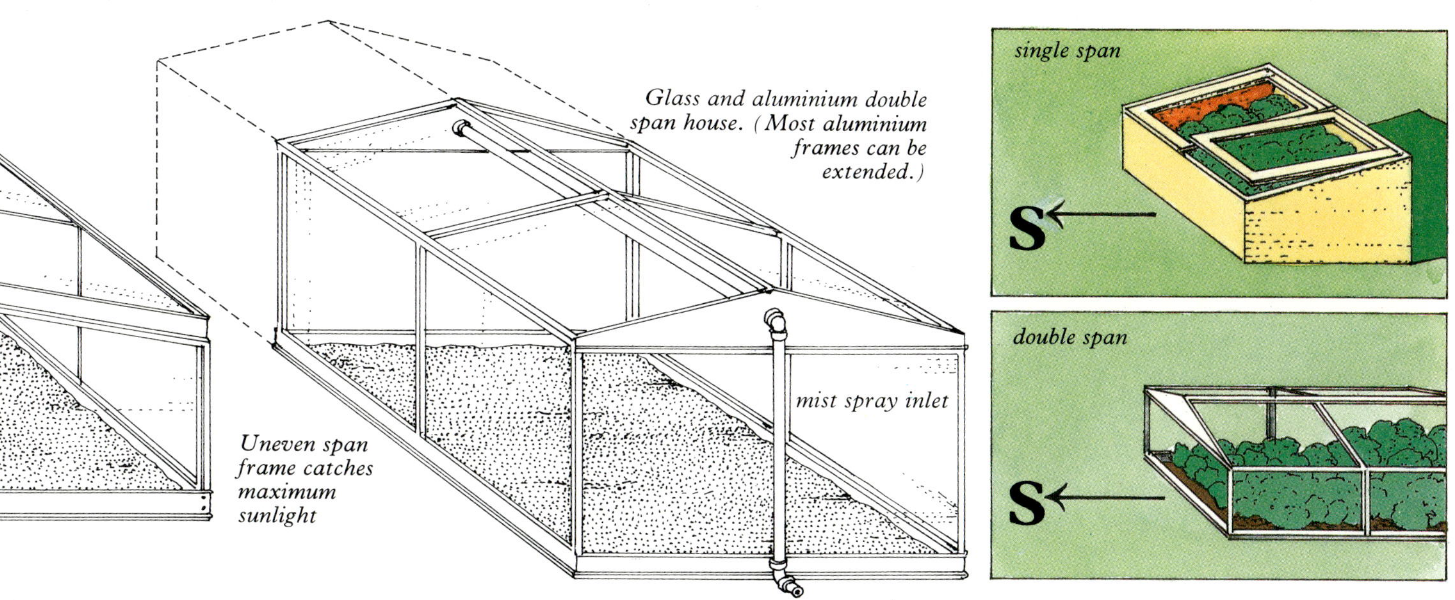

Glass and aluminium double span house. (Most aluminium frames can be extended.)

Uneven span frame catches maximum sunlight

Constructing a Dutch frame

A garden frame can easily be built by anyone who enjoys working with wood. For the type of frame shown below and on the opposite page, the ground area should measure no more than about 200 × 130 cm. Another factor influencing the size may be the lengths of timber available locally. If you want to cover a larger area, extend the frame sideways as shown at (A).

Floor boarding, particularly the type that is tongued and grooved, would give your structure extra firmness – it can sometimes be bought cheaply at demolition-contractors' yards. The corner supports (B) will probably have to be cut from new timber in a minimum thickness of 60 × 60 mm; use this module too for the other, thinner timber required for the glass lights.

Start by cutting and fitting the backboards to the support posts. Finish the frame and fit the centre beam (C) as shown. Add the side-battens (D), then complete the framework for the lights. Incidentally, if your Dutch frame is being made smaller than the one illustrated, your lights need only have a single pane. Otherwise insert the crosspieces (E). Use sprigs and putty to bed down the glass-panes.

Add two handles as shown. Fit two cleats – a length of rope can later be stretched between them and over the lights securing them in stormy weather. Finally, paint all the wood generously with a copper-based wood preservative. This treatment should be repeated every two years.

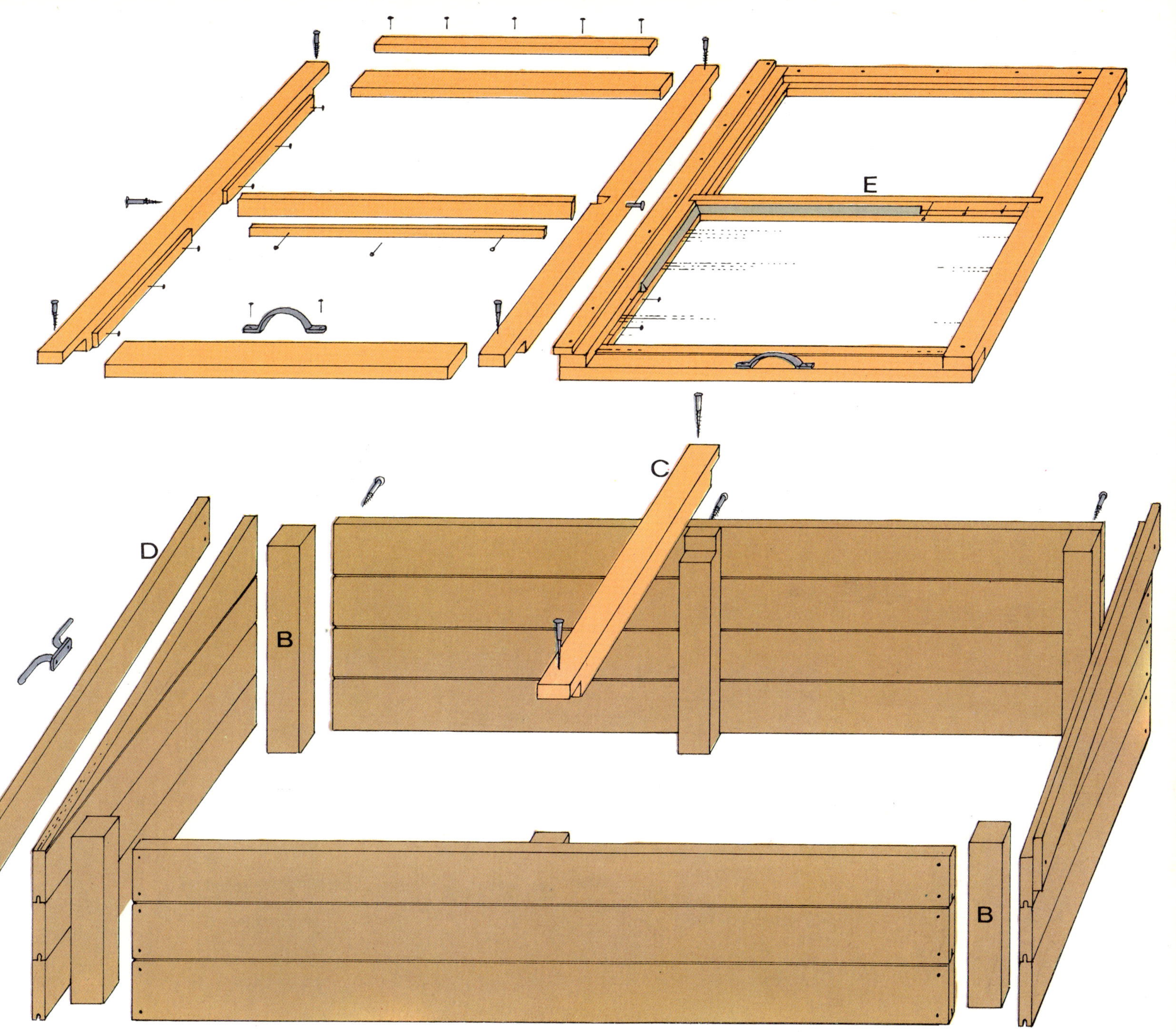
E
C
D
B
B

HEATING THE FRAME

By adding artificial heat to your frame you will be able to raise and harvest crops earlier than would normally be possible. And you will be providing a better environment for cuttings and seeds.

A frame can be heated with a small paraffin heater, but you must be careful about ventilation. As previously mentioned these heaters produce water vapour as they burn, making the atmosphere moist and humid.

Electric heating is more convenient, especially if your frame is close to a power supply, perhaps against the house wall or the greenhouse. You can use tubular heaters, but soil-warming cables are the more usual choice.

The cables come in various lengths, and your supplier will advise on the one best suited to your frame. You cannot cut or join them, so it is important to choose one that will give the right heat output for the area. They are usually supplied with a separate rod thermostat or with a tailstat located at the end of the cable.

If there is not already a convenient outdoor electricity supply, seek the advice of a qualified electrician. Special cables and damp-proof connections are required as well as other outdoor wiring requirements.

Before placing the soil-warming cable, dig out the soil to a depth of about 9in (23cm) below the surface soil and heap it to one side. Level the area and spread sand over the surface, raking it flat. Then lay the cable in gently looped parallel lines evenly spaced about 4in (10cm) apart. Do not allow the cables to touch or they will overheat. A safe way to keep the cable loops in position is to fix them with galvanised wire pegs. For further protection, lay a piece of galvanised netting over the area before covering it all with about 2in (5cm) of sand. Place the thermostat just above the sand before covering the surface with a loam-based or soil-less compost. Do not cover the cable with peat alone – it will dry out rapidly and can lead to serious overheating.

To warm the air in the frame, and as extra frost protection, supplementary cables can be fixed to the sides of the frame. Spring-clip them to the sides of a wooden frame, or on to free-standing wooden battens inside a frame with glass or metal sides.

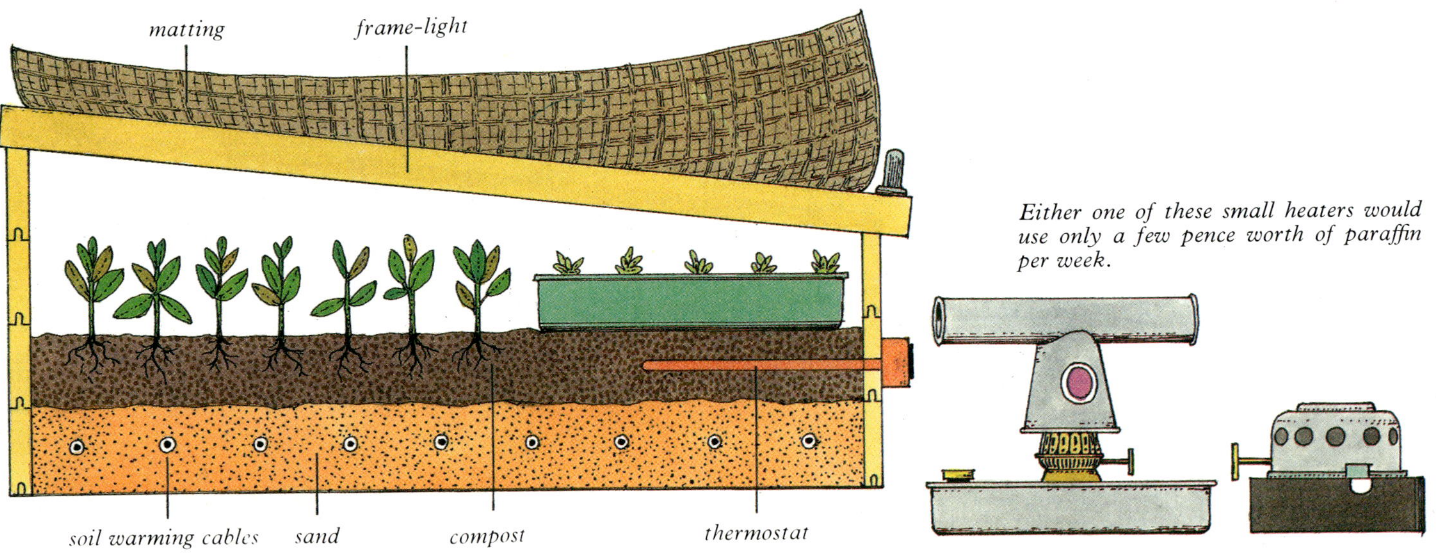

Either one of these small heaters would use only a few pence worth of paraffin per week.

It all starts with seeds

A seed is like a time-bomb just waiting to explode into growth – which it will do, under the right conditions of moisture, air, and warmth. Each seed is in fact a living, breathing organism that contains a plant embryo and enough food to start it off in life, however dried up it may appear.

When selecting seeds, it is a good idea to collect a good selection of catalogues to choose from, and to place your orders as early as possible. Although it is sometimes difficult, try to avoid the temptation of ordering more than you really need.

Seeds sold in paper packets have a shorter life than those packed in hermetically-sealed foil packets. The latter are packed under conditions of low humidity and moisture content, which greatly extends their life (although normal aging begins once the packet has been opened).

All seed packets should be stored in a dry, moisture-proof container such as a biscuit tin, and should be kept in a cool, frost-free place. A packet should only be opened when you are ready to sow the seeds. If any remain, turn the top over and seal it with an adhesive tape.

All seeds have a limited lifespan ranging from a matter of months to many years. An acacia seed has a tough watertight coat for protection and may remain viable for about 20 years. Others may lose their ability to germinate within months.

When starting seeds into growth, it really is worth using sterilised seed compost and clean containers. Also use clean glass or plastic to cover them.

Be sure to read the instructions carefully before dong anything.

THE COMPOST

For the majority of sowings, whether in pots or seed trays, a fine compost should be used. It does not matter much whether it is loam-based or soil-less. As seed compost only contains a little food, the seedlings should be pricked out as soon as possible. Always remember to turn over and cover the tops of the bags of compost if they are not stored in bins.

foil-packed

pelleted

paper-packed

stick seeds – right: *enlarged view of break-off section*

HOW TO SOW SEEDS

Place the compost into the tray or pot and strike off any excess so that it is level with the rim of the container. Gently firm round the sides and corners and then work into the middle to make sure that there are no air pockets. Then give the container a sharp tap to level the compost, or else use a wooden presser. The finished level should be about ½in (1cm) below the rim to allow room for watering.

An hour before sowing, thoroughly moisten the compost by using a watering-can fitted with a fine rose. Alternatively, gently lower the container into a large tray of water, and as soon as the top of the compost starts to darken, remove it. Always allow excess water to drain away before sowing your seeds, and never use water from the water butt as it can be heavily contaminated with disease spores.

TYPES OF SEED

Very fine dust-like seeds such as begonia, lobelia, and petunia, are difficult to sow evenly. So that they do not grow in clumps, mix a little silver sand with the seed and then shake the mixture evenly over the surface of the compost. These fine seeds are never covered with compost.

Seeds that are large enough to handle more easily, such as alyssum, celery and thyme, can be sown directly from the packet and should be spread evenly and thinly. Only just cover these with a little finely sifted compost.

Hairy or downy seeds such as statice, clematis or tagetes tend to stick together. It is worth mixing them with a little sharp sand to separate them before sowing. When sown, they should be covered with a thin layer of sifted compost and the surface lightly firmed

Large seeds, such as cyclamen, dahlia and sweetcorn, should be spaced in rows about 1in (2·5cm) apart, or sown in individual pots, singly or in groups. Cover the sifted compost to a depth of two to three times their diameter.

Seeds such as courgettes, broad beans and runner beans are best sown singly or in pairs in small pots. If both seeds germinate, the weaker seedling should be removed. Courgette seeds are flat and should be sown on their edges. All these large seeds will need to be covered by about 1in (2·5cm) of compost.

Pelleted seeds must be kept dry until they are sown. Then they will need to be kept constantly moist to break down the coating and allow the seed inside to germinate. They are fairly expensive, but can easily be spaced out in a seed tray and should be sown no deeper than their diameter.

F_1 hybrids are expensive because the seed has been carefully produced from special parent strains, and often pollinated by hand. The resulting seeds are exceptionally vigorous, and the plants very uniform. It is not worth saving second-generation F_1 hybrid seeds as the resulting plants are unlikely to be like the parent. You will have to buy fresh seed each year.

For those whose gardening skills are not yet fully developed, there are 'seed sticks'. Each stick (60 to a book) has three to four seeds adhering to the front, and they are treated with a fungicide to discourage damping off. They should be inserted into a pot or tray of compost to the depth indicated on the stick. This means that with precise spacing there will be less thinning to be done and the resulting plants should be strong and healthy.

Once the seeds have been sown, the pots or boxes should be covered with a sheet of glass and paper, or a piece of dark plastic (unless advised not to). Check the seeds daily, and as soon as they start to germinate remove the covering.

A good supply of air and a humid atmosphere should be maintained at all times. Check that the compost is moist, particularly soil-less composts as these can be difficult to moisten again. Use only clean water and spray gently but thoroughly with a fine mist sprayer.

If some seedlings start to collapse it may be due to damping off (caused by various fungi) and you should water with Cheshunt Compound (copper sulphate and ammonium carbonate).

PRICKING OUT SEEDLINGS

When the seedlings have developed two seed leaves, they should be pricked out into new seed trays. Hold the seedlings by their seed leaves, not their stems, and lever them out gently with the aid of a pencil or a plastic plant label. If, by any chance, two or three seedlings come out at the same time, gently separate and shake them to remove excess compost.

Make a hole sufficiently large to take the roots, with the seed leaves just above the compost. If the roots are rather long, make a small trench and lay the roots along it.

Firm the seedlings in gently, being careful not to touch the stem. They should be evenly spaced in rows, about 1–2in (2·5–5cm) apart. Gently water them in and shade them from bright sunlight for a few days.

Seedlings that have been pricked out will be able to withstand slightly lower temperatures than those necessary for germination.

LABELLING

Correctly naming and dating plants is essential. Memory is a poor substitute, and it is so easy to forget exactly which seed tray contains which seeds. You may also find it useful to note down the colours.

Mark each tray or pot carefully, and when the plants are finally set out in the garden label them there as well. Then you will have the answer if a friend asks for the name, and it makes it easier for recording their progress in a diary for future reference.

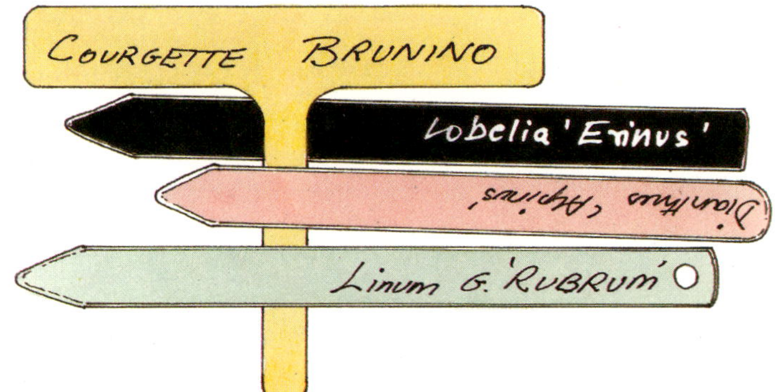

Increasing your plants

Propagating your own plants is a very enjoyable activity, and a cheap way to stock a garden or greenhouse. By growing from cuttings, you will be able to obtain exact replicas, or 'clones', of the parent plants. And cuttings will usually give you adult plants much sooner than growing from seed.

If you have a plant that has grown rather large and bushy and is not flowering quite as vigorously as it used to, it is a good idea to start again by taking cuttings from it. However, the younger the parent plant is, the faster the cutting will usually root. You can pass on the remaining cuttings to friends who will probably return the compliment. This way, in no time at all, you will have a good selection of sturdy young plants at minimal cost.

You should always choose a healthy plant for cuttings, and select sturdy shoots. Try to choose non-flowering growth, but if you have left it a bit late in the season and have to take a flowering shoot, remove all flowers and buds. Small 2–5in (5–12·5cm) long lateral growths (sideshoots) provide the best material for the majority of greenhouse plants.

When taking cuttings, always use a clean, sharp knife or a razor-blade so that you do not bruise the stem. Then dip the prepared base of the cutting into a rooting hormone powder or liquid to encourage roots to develop more quickly. If you use a preparation containing a fungicide it will also help to prevent the base from rotting before it roots.

A cutting needs moisture, light, and warmth. If the air is too dry, too much moisture will be lost from the leaves by transpiration. The leaves may wilt and dry out before roots have developed, so adequate humidity is important. Cuttings will usually root most readily in a humid atmosphere with generous bottom heat in an otherwise fairly cool environment. If it is too warm, the tip of the cutting will grow without roots being formed.

A cutting compost should be free-draining, and this can be achieved by using equal parts (by volume) of peat and coarse washed sand. Alternatively, use equal parts (by volume) of peat and sand or perlite. Or you can use vermiculite or a gritty seed compost. As there are no significant nutrients in these composts, the cuttings must be given an occasional weak liquid feed once they have rooted, and be potted up as soon as possible.

Cuttings should always rest in the bottom of a hole made by a dibber and be firmed in gently so that there are no air pockets, otherwise the roots that form will wither and die. If several cuttings are to be rooted in a single pot, insert them around the edge as this provides good drainage and better conditions.

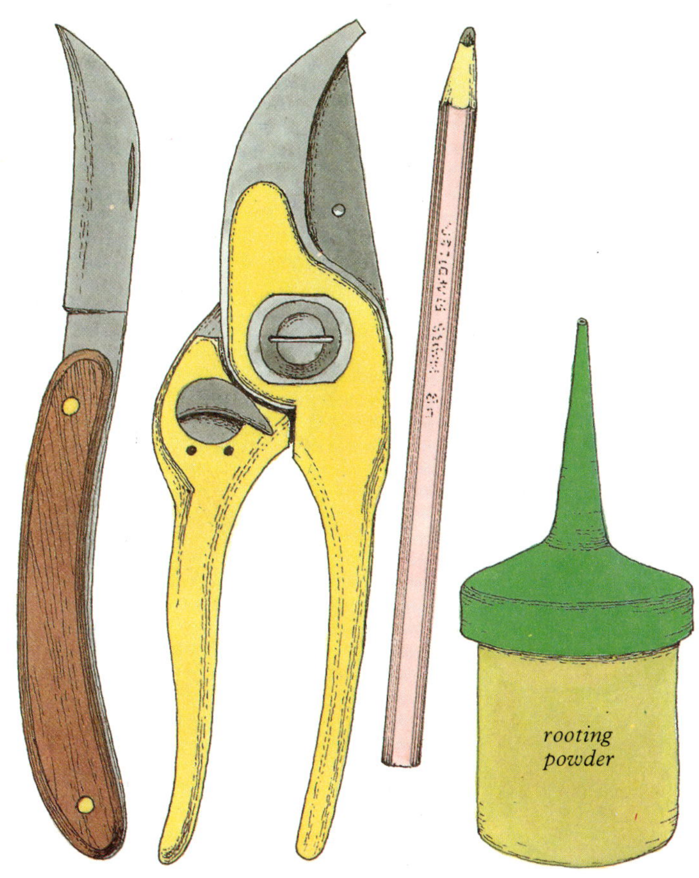

SOFTWOOD CUTTINGS

Softwood cuttings are taken from the current season's growth in spring or summer. They should be gathered early in the morning when they are turgid (not flagging from summer heat), and the cuttings prepared and inserted into cutting compost before they wilt.

Each shoot should be trimmed cleanly just below a leaf joint, to make it about 2–3in (5–7·5cm) long. The lower leaves should be removed, as buried leaves tend to rot and cause disease.

After dipping in a hormone rooting preparation, if used, insert it to about one-third of its length and firm into the compost. Water with a fungicide if one was not present in the rooting preparation. Then place in a propagator, ideally one with a mist unit (see page 41), as softwood cuttings need high humidity to prevent wilting. Most kinds prefer bottom heat of about 70°F (21°C). Alternatively, they can be inserted into trays or pots and covered with glass, clear plastic domes or polythene tents or bags supported on wire frames.

Shade them from bright sunlight, otherwise the leaves will wilt and scorch.

As soon as the shoots have rooted, generally between three and five weeks later although there is a wide variation, they should be hardened off gradually to the normal greenhouse atmosphere. Once hardened, they should be potted up without delay.

HALF-RIPE CUTTINGS

Half-ripe cuttings are taken in mid to late summer when the current season's growth has started to harden at the base. The shoot should usually be about 6in (15cm) long. Strip all leaves from the lower half to one-third of the stem, and if it has a soft tip, pinch this out.

Trim the shoot cleanly and neaten the base by cutting it off to immediately below a leaf joint.

Some shrubby subjects can be propagated from heel cuttings. With these a heel of older wood is removed with the cutting by gently pulling the shoot downwards to remove a sliver of the main stem with it. If there is a tail extending beyond the woody part it should be trimmed off cleanly.

Do not forget to dip the prepared bases into a hormone preparation before firming them into the cutting compost. These cuttings are not so susceptible to rot, so you do not normally need to use a fungicide.

Half-ripe cuttings will root in much cooler conditions, either in a propagator with a little bottom heat or in a covered garden frame. Spray them daily in warm bright weather and lightly shade them from the sun. They will have rooted by the autumn and should then be fed to encourage vigorous growth – but stop feeding before the cold weather sets in.

LEAF BLADE CUTTINGS

Some greenhouse plants, such as *Begonia rex* and streptocarpus, can be propagated from young, well-developed healthy leaves. They can be rooted at almost any time, but respond most readily in the warmer months.

To propagate *Begonia rex*, place the leaf upside down on a level surface, and carefully nick the main veins with a sharp, clean knife or razor-blade, every 2in (5cm), being careful not to crush the leaf. Lay the leaf cut-side downwards on moist cutting compost and peg it down with wire staples or scatter small pebbles over the surface to ensure good contact.

Alternatively, the leaf can be cut into small pieces about 1 in (2·5cm) square. Make sure that a vein runs through its centre, and that the pieces are pegged flat against the compost.

Streptocarpus leaf cuttings can have the main vein nicked on the underside, and be treated in a similar way to *Begonia rex*. Or they can be cut into 2in (5cm) strips, which are inserted into the compost in an upright position with the bottom $\frac{1}{2}$in (1cm) buried in the compost. If the leaves flop, prop them up with short sticks (old matchsticks will do). Soon new plantlets will emerge and when the plants are potted up the parent leaf can be cut into sections where there is new growth.

LEAF PETIOLE CUTTINGS

New saintpaulias (African violets) and peperomias can be started at any time of the year provided recently matured new leaves are available.

Remove a leaf from the plant and with a clean knife, cut the leaf stalk (petiole) so that there is a 2in (5cm) piece attached to the leaf blade. Dip the base into rooting powder and insert the petiole into the prepared cutting compost at a shallow angle, and firm it gently. Continue in this fashion until the container is filled, then spray with a fungicide before placing the container in a propagator or covering it with a sheet of glass or a polythene bag. Shade it from direct sunlight.

Once the plantlets have formed, gradually harden them in the greenhouse and then pot them up individually.

INTERNODAL CUTTINGS

New plants can be raised from internodal cuttings. Each cutting is taken by slicing through the stem an inch (25mm) above and below a leaf joint that has a plump bud (or buds). The severed piece of stem is then planted horizontally with the bud just covered. The leaf should protrude above the surface of the compost. A new shoot and roots will soon form from bud and it should be potted up immediately.

ROOT CUTTINGS

Root cuttings are an easy way in which to increase herbaceous plants such as anchusa, *Phlox* and anemone and are best taken in spring.

The plants should be dug up and roots of average thickness severed from the parent plant. They should then be cut into 2–3 in (5–7cm) lengths. Evenly space them in rows over the top of the compost in a seed tray. Then cover the pieces with $\frac{1}{2}$ in (1cm) of sifted compost and cover the tray with a clean sheet of glass. The tray can either be placed in a cold frame or in a cool part of a greenhouse. The cuttings will start to root after about six weeks.

AIR LAYERING

Tall-growing, leggy plants, such as rubber plants that have dropped their lower leaves, can be induced to grow roots on main stems or branches while still attached to the parent.

During spring or late summer if you want to increase your stock, select a straight healthy stem or a branch that is becoming woody. Make a long, slanting cut starting from below the node (where a leaf joins the stem) and upwards and towards the centre of the stem. This cut should be made about 9–12 in (23–30cm) from the tip of a strongly-growing side shoot. Use a really sharp knife and take your time, otherwise you may accidentally cut right through the stem.

Keep the incision open by inserting a sliver of wood or half a matchstick, then apply hormone rooting powder liberally to the cut surfaces (a paintbrush is useful for this). Tightly wrap the wound with wet, but not saturated, sphagnum moss, and wrap the ball of moss with a piece of clear polythene secured top and bottom with waterproof tape, or raffia.

If you do not trust yourself not to cut through the stem, you can remove a ring of bark about ½in (1cm) wide from just below a leaf joint instead. Use a rooting powder and bind the exposed ring with moss as already described.

Keep the plant in a warm, moist atmosphere, and water as usual. After a few months, you should be able to see some roots through the polythene. If in doubt, unwrap it and check; if rooting has not occurred, make sure that the polythene is well sealed again.

Once sufficient roots have formed, sever the new plant from the parent, then carefully undo the tape or raffia and remove the polythene. Cleanly cut away the stem to just below the roots, then gently loosen the moss ball and place the new plant in a 5–6in (12–15cm) pot filled with John Innes potting compost No 1. Hold the plant upright and gently firm the compost around the brittle roots.

The newly potted plant should be kept warm and shaded from bright sunlight until new growth begins.

Make an upward incision

or cut a 1cm ring out of the bark.

Apply hormone powder to the cut and pack the moss.

Cover with polythene.

Cut off branch when roots have formed.

RUNNERS

Plants such as the spider plant (chlorophytum) and mother-of-thousands (*Saxifraga stolonifera*) are easy to propagate, and they grow quickly. The saxifraga sends out strawberry-like runners, with miniature plantlets at the end, while the chlorophytum carries its plantlets at the ends of arching stems.

The plantlets will root readily if pegged down singly in 3in (7·5cm) pots filled with John Innes potting compost No 1. Sever them from the parent plant once they have rooted. Alternatively, you can remove the plantlets first, then root them in humid conditions in a propagator before potting up.

The succulent *Kalanchoe daigremontiana* has miniature plantlets along the edges of the leaves. These will form roots while still on the parent and simply need potting up.

OFFSETS

Some bulbs readily produce small bulbs called offsets. These can be potted up in small pots or trays. They may take a year or two to flower, but will be quicker to mature than most bulbs raised from seed and cheaper than buying flowering-sized bulbs.

Cacti also produce offsets, but these are miniature versions of the parent plant attached to the main stem – not bulbs. These offsets are easily detached and will soon root if potted up.

BULB SCALES

Scaling is a form of propagation used to increase lilies. In autumn after they have flowered, lift the bulbs and carefully remove a few scales from the basal plate of healthy plants before replanting them. Insert the scales upright about $1\frac{1}{2}$in (4cm) apart in a tray filled with cutting compost. If kept at about 65°F (18°C) and humid, roots and small 'bulblets' should start to form after six to eight weeks.

Another way to root the scales is to place them in a polythene bag half filled with a damp – but not too wet – seed compost. Blow air into the bag before sealing the top and then leave it in a warm place for about six to eight weeks. By that time roots should have started to form and they can be potted up into small pots, with the tips just showing.

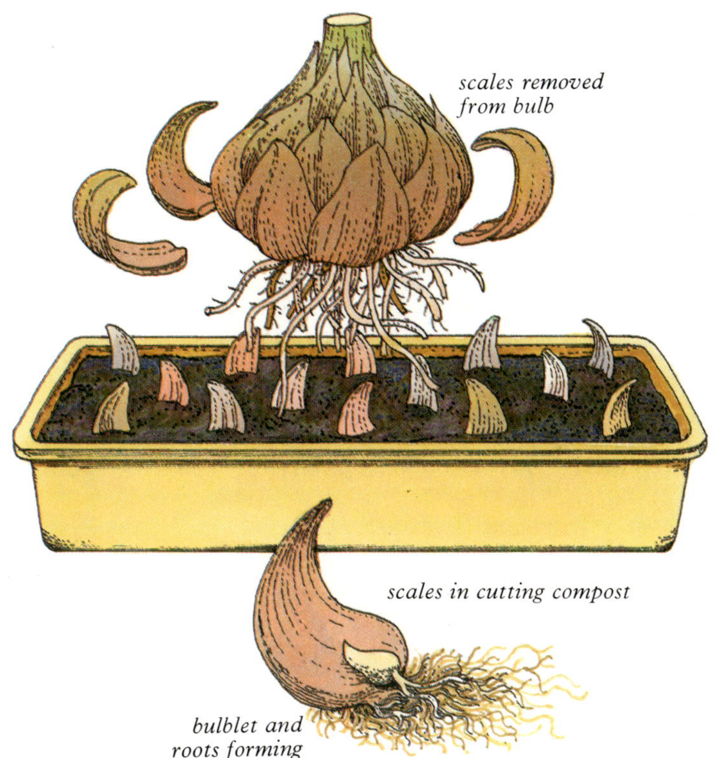

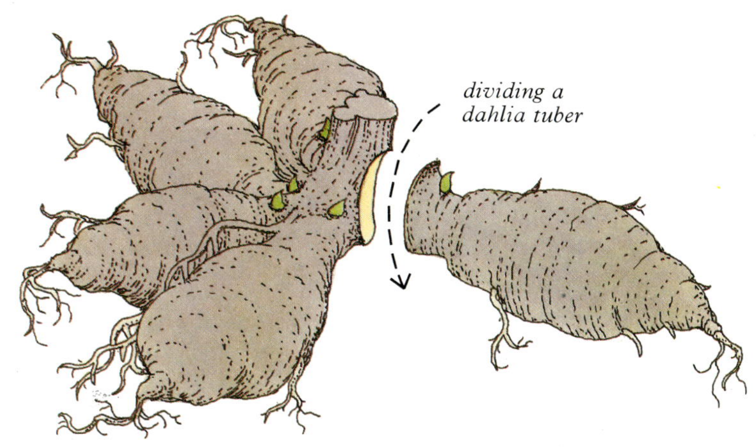

DIVISION

Perennial plants like dahlias (which you may be starting off in the greenhouse) and tuberous begonias can be divided to form new plants. As dahlias have eyes at the base of the old stem, not on the tubers, you must make sure each piece has a bit of old stem when you cut it with a sharp knife. Tuberous begonias can be cut up into several portions, each one having at least one bud or shoot.

Whenever you cut tubers it is best to dust the exposed surfaces with flowers of sulphur or spray with a fungicide to reduce the risk of disease.

Most clump-forming plants with fibrous roots – such as African violets (saintpaulias) – can be divided simply by teasing the old plant into small pieces and potting them up.

General cultivation

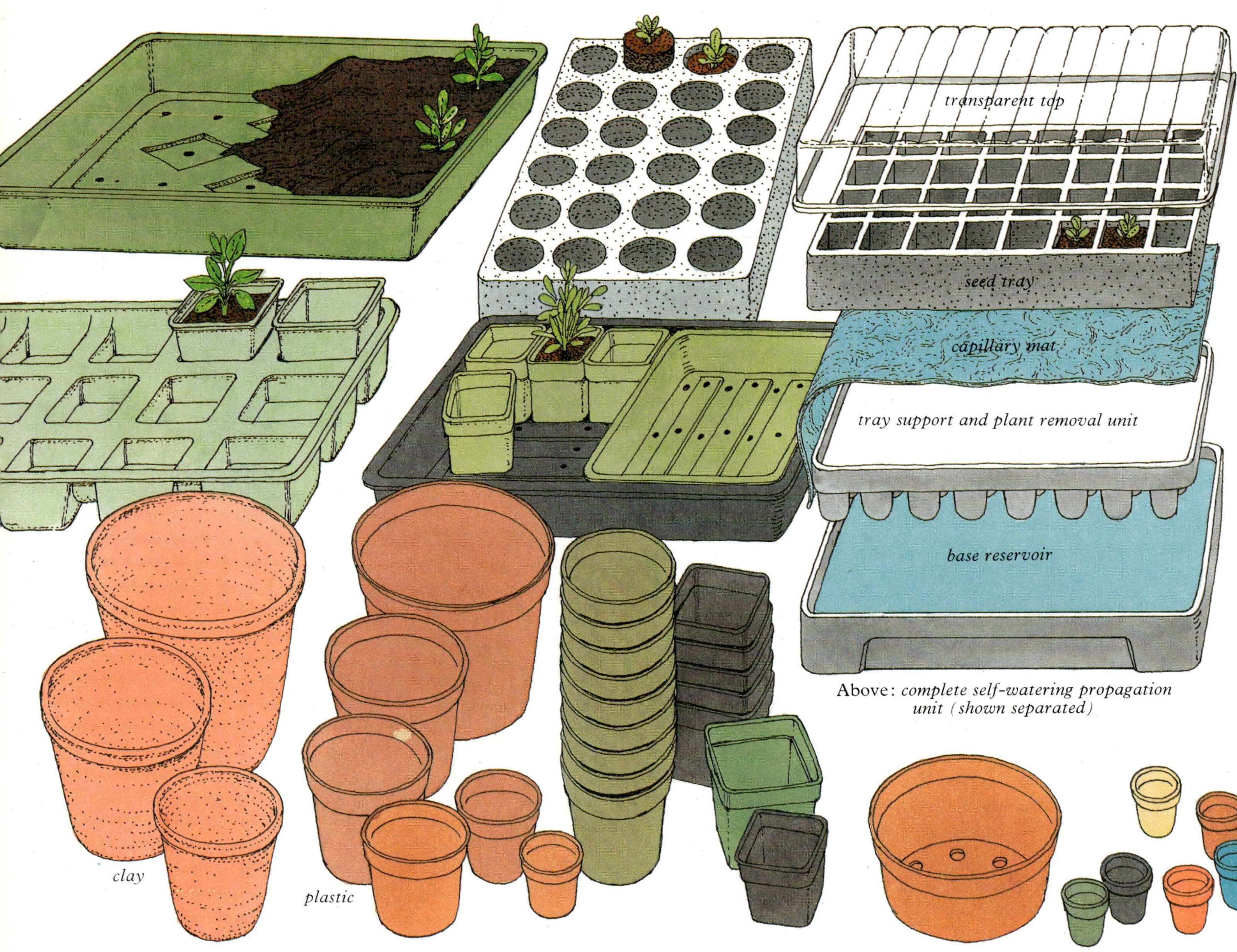

Above: *complete self-watering propagation unit (shown separated)*

CONTAINERS

Plant containers are available in a wide range of sizes and shapes as well as many materials – clay, plastic, bitumen-paper, expanded polystyrene, and peat, for example. There is sure to be a container to suit the job you have in mind.

Seed trays are used mainly for sowing seeds and pricking out seedlings (to give them more room to develop and to provide a richer compost), but they can also be useful for small cuttings. Wooden trays have various drawbacks, so it is best to buy the plastic type. Moulded plastic trays incorporating drainage holes are more practical to use; they are easily cleaned and stacked, and can be bought in standard or half-tray sizes – the latter being useful when there are only a few seeds to be sown or seedlings to be pricked out.

Plastic trays are made in various grades. Some are very thin and flexible, and although they are cheap, they may be more expensive in the long run because they are easily broken if not handled with care. The more rigid types are more expensive initially but will last a lot longer.

Expanded polystyrene 'trays' are excellent for raising bedding and vegetable plants. Their insulating property encourages a good root growth. Trays with individual compartments allow plants to develop their own compact rootballs so that they will not receive a check when planted out. Another advantage is that the hole in the base of each cell allows drainage and easy removal of the plants by placing the tray onto a special key plate with upright pegs. The key plate should be placed on a flat surface so that the pegs point upwards, and the tray with its plants held over the pegs and gently pushed down so that all the plants pop out. These trays can be used over and over again, and you need only one key plate to serve any number of them.

You can also buy trays made of thin plastic, that come complete with clear plastic lids. Some of these trays are divided into a number of compartments in which individual seeds can be sown, others are carrying trays with a small square tapering pot which fits into each compartment. These sectionalised trays are widely used by commercial growers.

Finally, there is the complete expanded polystyrene propagator unit. This consists of a deep tray, the key plate, a strip of capillary matting, and the plant tray itself which is covered with a clear rigid plastic dome. The unit can be used to raise plants in the greenhouse or on a windowsill.

Clay pots with their traditional texture are a joy to handle but the fact that they are heavy, easily broken if dropped, and more expensive, is responsible for the success of the plastic types. Many gardeners prefer to use clay pots when rooting cuttings or plunging plants in beds of ash, as clay is porous and allows the roots to breathe. And being porous, the soil will dry out not only from the top, but from the sides as well, so there are fewer problems caused by overwatering. Because of their weight, clay pots are also good for top-heavy plants, and are more stable in windy conditions.

Clay pots should always be soaked in water before use, and they also need to be crocked (a few pieces of broken flower pots or pebbles placed in the bottom) before being filled with compost. Do not forget that clay pots tend to dry out more rapidly than plastic ones in warm weather. They also accumulate slime and algae easily and are best avoided where trickle irrigation or mist propagation is employed or when capillary matting is being used.

It is probably best not to clean the pots in a disinfectant because the chemicals may be retained in the microscopic pores of the clay; simply wash and scrub them thoroughly in warm, soapy water.

Plastic pots are widely used by commercial growers and amateur gardeners. They can be round or square, and are usually coloured green, black or terracotta. Brighter colours are available but they tend to look rather garish and their intensity competes with the natural colour of the plant.

Pot diameters range from about 2in (5cm) to over 12in (30cm). Square pots are not made in very large sizes, but their shape is extremely practical when raising young plants or cuttings because they can be packed together more tightly than round ones.

Plastic pots are easy to clean and stack when empty, and are also light in weight. They do not break so easily when dropped, but with age, and exposure to strong sunlight, they will become brittle. Alkathene pots are more expensive, but last longer and are therefore a good choice for large pots which are to be stood outdoors. Plastic pots are not porous, so the compost will not dry out so quickly and care should be taken to avoid waterlogging. They are however made with a number of small drainage holes, so there is no need to crock them.

The cheapest of all pots are old plastic containers such as yogurt cartons, margarine tubs, and plastic cups. You will have to punch some drainage holes in the bottom, but otherwise they are perfectly serviceable where appearances do not matter.

Fold-flat polythene pots are small, black, lightweight bags that open up into pots that are very useful for short-term cultivation. They are widely used in nurseries and garden centres. They are not worth saving for re-use as they are cheap to buy. Until you get the hang of them, they can be rather awkward to fill with compost, and care must be taken to fill the corners to avoid air pockets.

Always remove the bags before planting. Plastic does not rot, and root growth would be severely inhibited.

Bitumen pots are usually made from vegetable matter and bitumen. These small black pots are generally used for starting off seedlings that are to be planted outside and because the roots grow through the thin wall (which will eventually decay), the pot does not have to be removed before planting. Consequently, there is little root disturbance.

Red-coloured bitumen containers about 23cm (9in) in diameter are widely used for ring culture and should last for at least eight months.

Compressed peat blocks are relatively expensive and can be bought singly, in strips, or in blocks. Plants grown in these pots will have little root disturbance when they are potted on or planted out because the entire unit is planted. Eventually the pot will rot away if it is kept moist.

It is a good idea to place peat pots on capillary matting so that they do not dry out.

Being so fragile, peat pots should not be handled too often, otherwise they will soon disintegrate.

One type of peat pot comes in the form of a flat compressed peat disc encased in a thin mesh net. The disc expands when it is soaked in water and has a hole in the centre to allow a single seed to be sown or a single cutting to be inserted. Roots will grow through the walls, so the whole unit should be planted or potted before they become too prominent.

It is essential that the discs are kept moist, but not saturated, because once they have dried out they are very difficult to moisten again.

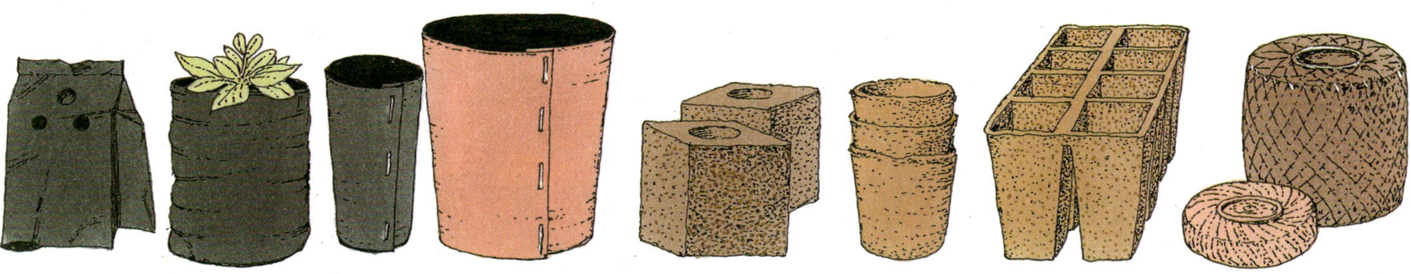

ALL ABOUT POTTING

There is often confusion about terms like 'potting', 'potting on' and 'repotting'. Potting – sometimes termed potting up – is the initial potting; potting on involves moving the plant into a larger pot; repotting, in this book, means putting the plant back into a pot of the same size; top-dressing is a technique used to add a little fresh compost without disturbing the plant.

Potting

Cuttings should be potted as soon as they are well rooted and making steady growth.

Always water the cuttings first and loosen them by knocking the edge of the pot or tray against a hard surface. Then, with a blunt pencil or a dibber, ease out the cuttings while keeping the rootball as large as possible.

Place each cutting in a 3in (7·5cm) pot and check that the base of the stem will be level with the surface of the compost, about $\frac{1}{2}$in (1 cm) below the rim of the pot. Then trickle potting compost around the roots, and give the pot a gentle tap to settle the compost and eliminate any air pockets. Roots should be well covered and the cutting placed in the centre of the pot. Add more compost if needed, firm lightly and tap the pot again to level the surface before watering.

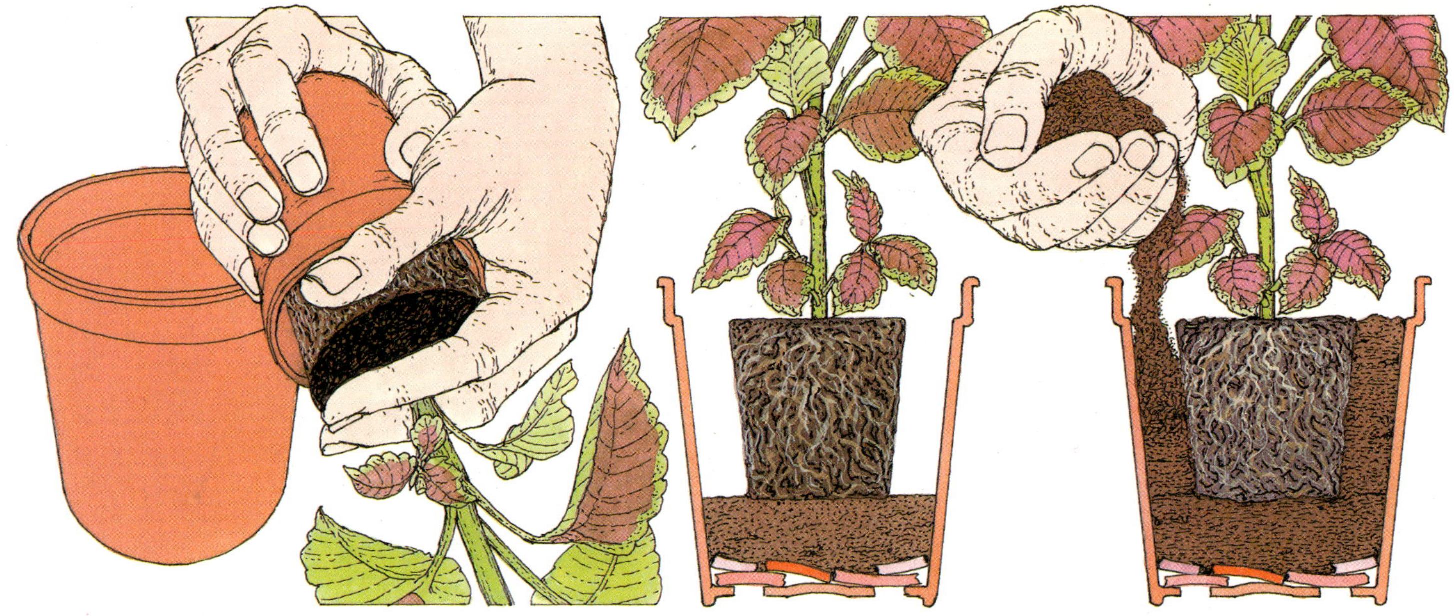

Potting on

When a plant becomes top-heavy, or the roots are matted and pressed tightly against the inside of the pot, it needs to be potted on into a container an inch or so larger than the present pot. Roots emerging through the drainage holes are a timely indication that a plant needs to be potted on, although plants on capillary matting will tend to root through sooner than others.

Before potting on, water the plant but do not soak it. Then prepare a clean pot by lining the bottom with fresh, slightly moist compost, remembering to crock it if necessary.

To knock the pot off the rootball, place a finger on either side of the stem, then turn the pot over. Either give the pot a sharp tap on the sides, or knock the rim against a hard surface.

Place the plant in the new pot and check that the surface is about $\frac{1}{2}$in (1cm) below the rim of the pot to allow for watering. Fill the gap between roots and pot with moist compost, making sure that there are no air pockets. Then firm the surface and water lightly.

Repotting

When a plant has reached maturity and its ultimate size, it may need to be repotted each spring.

Before knocking off the pot (see potting on), prepare a new one the same size by lining the bottom with fresh compost. If you want to re-use the same pot, make sure it is really clean before replacing the plant.

Having separated the plant and pot, gently scrape away some of the compost until it has been reduced by about a quarter and cut off any old and matted roots. Then place the rootball in the prepared pot and fill the gap with fresh compost, again making sure that there are no air pockets. Finally, firm the surface of the compost before watering.

Top-dressing

Plants that resent root disturbance or which have been in the same pot for a year or more, will need top-dressing in early spring before growth begins again. Carefully scrape away some of the surface compost and replace it with a fresh compost.

HOW TO SUPPORT PLANTS

If you are developing 'green fingers', your plants will develop too; in fact some may grow to such a size that they will need to be supported by artificial means. Climbing plants will need permanent support, while tomato and cucumber plants will need a strong temporary support.

Well supported plants benefit from a less restricted flow of food and water, and by growing upright they take up less space, have good access to light, and allow the air to circulate more freely.

Attaching vertical or horizontal wires to wood-framed greenhouses presents no problems. Aluminium greenhouses, on the other hand, need to be equipped with special bolts and brackets that can be slotted into the glazing bars to carry the wires.

Bamboo or plastic-coated canes are useful for borders and should be inserted when planting, one to a plant. Because bamboo canes are hollow, they need to be cleaned with a disinfectant at the end of each season to control pests and diseases.

Split canes are short, thin pieces of cane that have been split lengthways and can be used singly or fan-shaped to support plants in pots.

Supports for growing bags: plants can be supported on free-standing metal frames, or by securing them with soft string or twine. One end of the string is usually anchored to the ground (but not through the growing bag) by means of a wire hook, or it can be loosely tied round the stem just below the plant's first true leaf. The string is then loosely wound in a clockwise direction up and along the rest of the stem and the other end attached to the greenhouse structure or to a wire. Avoid pulling the string too taut, and leave a little extra on the end for further adjustment.

Twigs and brushwood can be used to support pot-grown dwarf beans, young climbers, and bushy plants such as schizanthus. Insert them in the pots between the young seedlings, which will grow through and conceal them.

1 *Split canes*
2 *Twigs or brushwood*
3 *Canes tied to wires*
4 *Plastic-covered metal frame supports plants in growing bag*

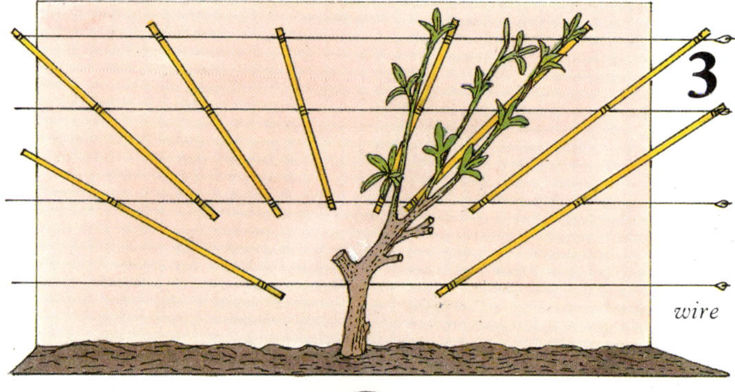

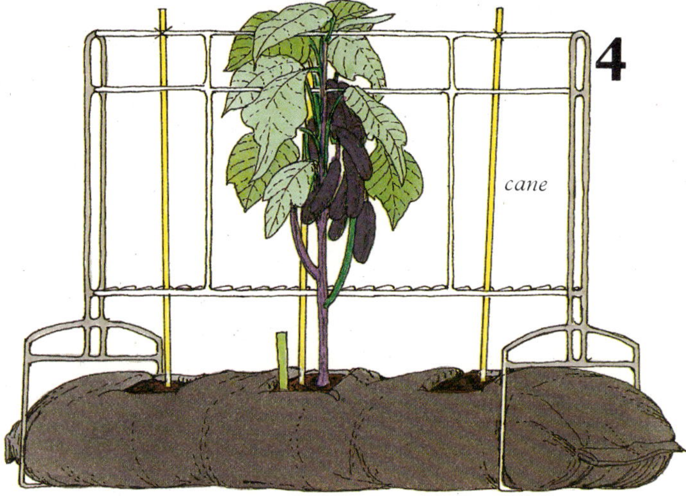

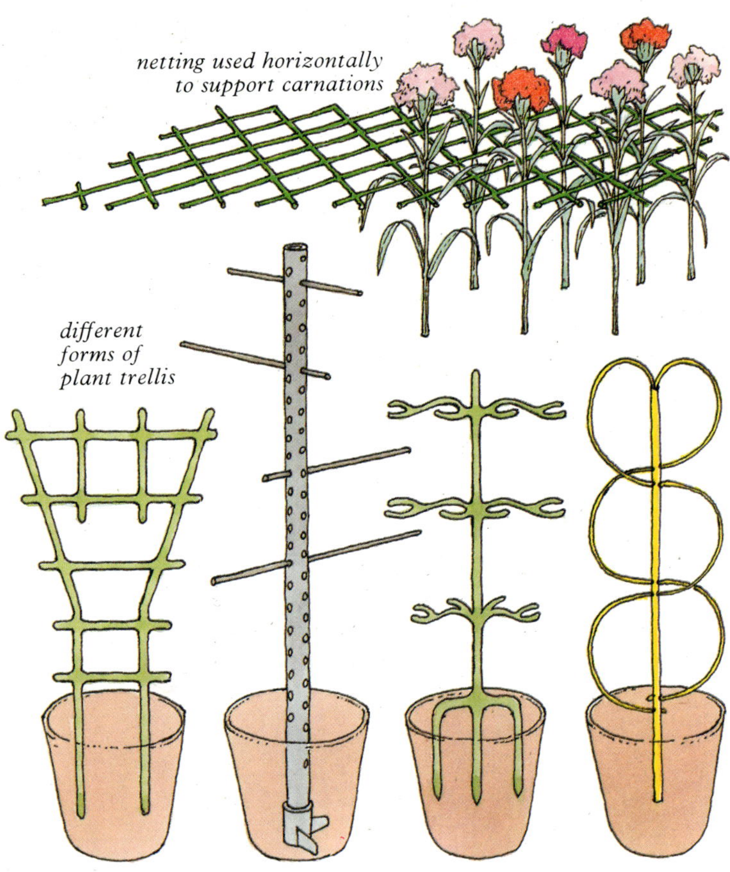

Netting either made wholly from plastic or from plastic-covered wire can be bought in varying mesh sizes. It should be attached securely to the greenhouse framework before the plants are put into position.

Use plastic-covered wire for perennial climbing plants as it will last longer than the weaker plastic mesh which may deteriorate after a few years' exposure to strong sunlight. But thin plastic mesh is often stretched over staging and borders for carnations to grow through, or it can be used to support heavy fruits like melons.

Climbing frames and plant trellises are available in metal, plastic, or wood. There are many shapes and sizes, suitable for supporting and displaying a large range of pot-grown plants.

Lengths of wire often make helpful supports in the greenhouse. Choose galvanised or plastic-coated wire to avoid rusting. Climbers and melon plants can be trained along wires, which must be kept taut to prevent sagging. Upright canes can also be tied to fixed wires to support tomatoes and cucumbers.

Pot hangers are fittings for hanging up pots – made from metal, plastic or decorative string-work. They need to be attached to a suitable horizontal bar. Take care that water does not drip onto plants standing below them.

Twist ties are a quick and convenient way of securing plants, and are made from plastic or butiminised paper strengthened by a thin wire running through the centre. They are available in pre-cut lengths or on spools and have many uses, but care should be taken not to twist the ends too tightly when linking a soft or brittle stem to a support.

Wire rings are split galvanised rings that are used to support long-stemmed plants such as carnations against a central cane.

wire
string
string
pot hanger
open basket hangs from a swivel bracket
wire and eye hook
angle bracket on glazing bar
hook & eye fitted to glazing bar
typical slide-hook in glazing bar
wire ring
1
twist tie
2
3
cane
calyx ring
hook

FORCING PLANTS

'Forcing' is simply a method employed to induce plants to fruit or flower earlier or later than their normal cycle. Rhubarb and chicory, for instance, are very popular with gardeners and if a temperature of 55°F (15°C) can be maintained in the greenhouse throughout the winter, they can be conveniently placed out of the way under the staging.

Rhubarb

During late autumn, dig up a number of two-year-old crowns and spread them on the surface of the soil for a few days so that they become frosted. Then pack them tightly together in a deep box and fill up the remaining spaces with peat. Water the box well before laying hessian sacks over the top, as the crowns must be in complete darkness. The crowns and compost must be kept moist, so check the box at least once a week.

In about eight weeks you will be able to harvest tender young sticks of rhubarb at a time when they are normally unobtainable.

After forcing, the exhausted crowns should be discarded.

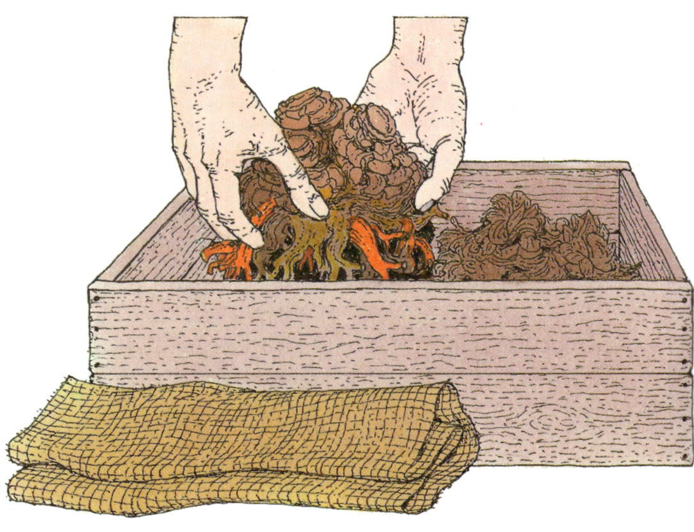

Chicory Roots

Roots should be lifted during late autumn and their tops trimmed off to within $\frac{1}{2}$in (1cm) of the crown. Then place the roots in a box of dry sand and store in a frostproof place until needed.

Towards the end of late autumn, put three or four roots in a large plastic pot or tightly pack a few more together in a box. Fill the spaces with moist peat but leave $\frac{1}{2}$in (1cm) of the crown above the surface of the soil. Water and cover with an inverted pot or box of the same size. Place a sheet of black polythene over the top before storing under the staging. It is essential that all light is excluded, otherwise the new shoots will become yellow and taste bitter. The chicons will be ready for cutting three or four weeks later.

For a continuous supply of chicons, pot up new roots at weekly intervals. The roots should be discarded after forcing.

Herbs

Parsley, mint, and a clump of chives, can be potted up in John Innes potting compost No 1 and grown on in the greenhouse to provide fresh leaves for most of the winter.

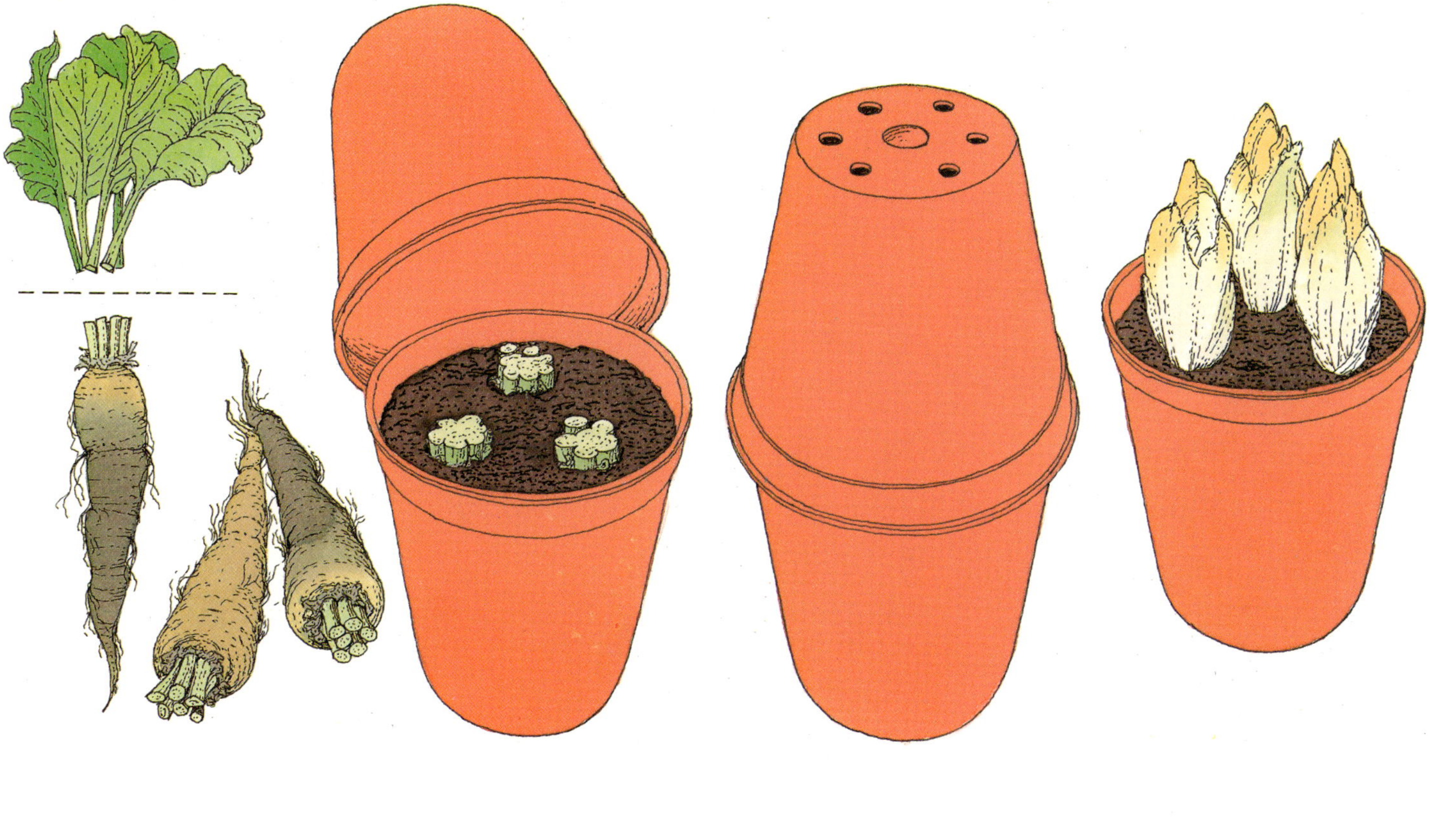

Composts

When plants grow so well in ordinary soil in the garden there may seem little point – at first thought – in using a special compost for pot plants. But a plant growing in the garden is able to develop a large root system to search out water and nutrients. When it is grown in a pot, the roots are confined and must therefore be provided with a richer compost and an effective means of drainage.

In the old days, gardeners used to mix up their own composts from whatever was to hand on a hit-or-miss basis; sometimes with success, but often with disastrous results. Then in 1939, after much research and experiment, W. J. C. Lawrence and J. Newell of the John Innes Horticultural Institute in Britain published a book called 'Seed and Potting Composts'. It was to revolutionise the gardening scene and John Innes composts still play an important role in pot-plant cultivation.

Two basic formulae were devised, one for seed germination and one for potting. The potting compost comes in three grades each containing an increasing amount of nutrient: Nos 1, 2, and 3.

Over the last few years, however, it has become increasingly difficult to obtain suitable loam and this has encouraged the development of peat-based composts.

Soil-less composts tend to dry out more rapidly and are quite difficult to wet once they do. Store them in a cool, dark place so that they remain slightly moist.

Peat-based composts will need regular feeding, and this can be particularly important for long-term plants in pots. Another disadvantage is that peat is light, so tall plants may overbalance in a peat-based compost.

If you have a supply of good loam you can make your own John Innes compost. But it must be sterilised, and it may not be worth the cost of a steriliser if you only need a small quantity each year. If you do use enough to justify making your own, follow the recipe given below.

Composts should always be mixed on a scrupulously clean surface to avoid contamination from pests and diseases. Turn the material over three or four times with a clean shovel (if you are preparing a small amount, you can use your hands). It is not advisable to store the composts for longer than a month as chemical reactions take place that can actually inhibit germination or damage newly potted plants.

In mixing the sometimes large amounts required, it is useful to remember that an ordinary bucket will usually contain about 2 gallons (9 litres). To convert still larger amounts from imperial to metric use this table:

8 gallons is approximately 36 litres
4 gallons is approximately 18 litres
2 gallons is approximately 9 litres

John Innes seed compost
2 parts sieved, sterilised loam
1 part peat
1 part coarse horticultural sand or grit
All parts by volume
To every four buckets of mixed compost add:
1½oz (42g) superphosphate of lime (18% phosphoric acid)
¾oz (21g) ground chalk or limestone

John Innes potting compost
7 parts sieved, sterilised loam
3 parts peat
2 parts coarse horticultural sand or grit
All parts by volume
To every four buckets of mixed compost add:
For JI No 1:
4oz (113g) John Innes base fertiliser*
¾oz (21g) ground chalk or limestone
For JI No 2:
8oz (226g) John Innes base fertiliser*
1½oz (42g) ground chalk or limestone
For JI No 3:
12oz (340g) John Innes base fertiliser*
2¼oz (63g) ground chalk or limestone

As a very approximate guide, No 1 is suitable for pricking out or potting up seedlings and cuttings; No 2 can be used for potting on most plants; No 3 is suitable for the final potting of 'hungry' plants such as chrysanthemums.

If you want to grow lime-hating plants, the mixture will have to be modified and it is easier to buy a special mixture for any acid-loving plants.

*If you are unable to buy John Innes base fertiliser, you can make it yourself from:
2 parts hoof and horn (13% nitrogen)
2 parts superphosphate of lime (18% phosphoric acid)
1 part sulphate of potash (48% potash)
All parts by weight. The percentages given indicate the amount of active ingredient in each chemical.

For lime haters omit the ground chalk or limestone. To make the compost more acid you can add ¾oz (21g) of flowers of sulphur to every four buckets of mixed compost.

Do-it-yourself loamless composts

Peat-based composts are difficult to make at home unless you use a special fertiliser pack. This is because of the difficulty of providing trace elements in a suitable form.

If you want to make your own peat-based compost for potting, buy a peat-based fertiliser pack and follow the instructions.

Because seeds and cuttings do not need the same amount of fertiliser as mature plants and have less need of the trace elements initially, there is no reason why you should not try making your own seed and cutting compost.

Use equal parts (by volume) of peat and sand. Or you can substitute perlite or vermiculite for the sand. Use granular sphagnum peat, and sharp or coarse horticultural (lime-free) sand.

To every four buckets of compost add ½oz (14g) sulphate of ammonia, 1oz (28g) superphosphate of lime, ½oz (14g) sulphate of potash, and 4 oz (113g) ground chalk or limestone. Mix all the ingredients thoroughly.

Perlite is a sterile inert granular material of volcanic origin. It is light when dry, but increases its weight in water. It is particularly useful for ericaceous and lime-hating plants and for rooting cuttings.

Vermiculite is also a sterile inert material, formed of flakes of a form of mica. It is light in weight and water-retentive; yet it improves aeration and drainage. Some samples may be too alkaline for ericaceous and lime-hating plants.

For cuttings you can simply use a mixture of equal parts (by volume) of peat and sand/perlite/vermiculite, or perlite or vermiculite can be used on their own.

BLOCKING COMPOST

Blocking compost consists of a blend of moist sphagnum peat and balanced nutrients and should therefore not be mixed with any other material. It is sold in bags of various weights; if a block-making tool is not supplied, they are inexpensive to buy. Most block-making tools press out a single block, although some will produce multiples of three or four at a time.

In the greenhouse, the blocks are useful for raising early vegetable plants such as tomatoes, peppers, aubergines, and melons. They are not really suitable for root crops like carrots or parsnips. When the blocks are planted out later the plants will suffer little root damage and growth will not be checked.

Never allow peat blocks to dry out completely. If this does happen, water them thoroughly with a fine rose.

It is usual to sow several seeds in each block, then thin them to one if several germinate. It is however possible to retain several seedlings in one block for some vegetables, but spacings have to be adjusted when planting them out in the garden.

To prepare the blocks you will need a clean plastic washing-up bowl and ideally a pair of rubber gloves (preparation is a fairly messy business).

Decide roughly how many plants you want to grow, and then work out the amount of compost you will need. About $2\frac{1}{4}$ pints ($1\frac{1}{4}$ litres) of clean cold water added to 5 litres of compost will usually make about 25–30 blocks. Mix the compost thoroughly until it is

Add water to the compost until the mixture sticks together.

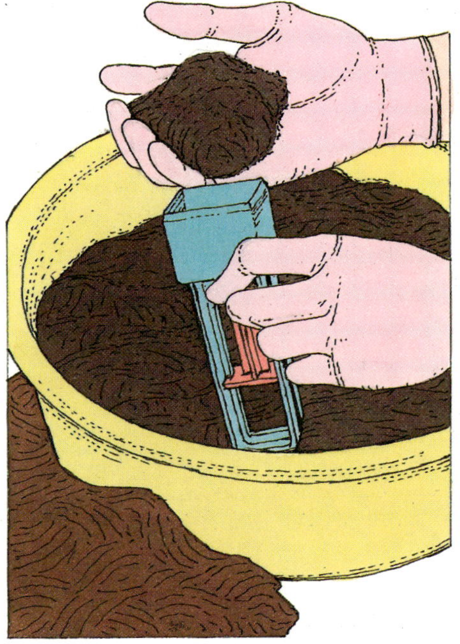

Fill the blocking tool with the moist compost.

Scrape off surplus to obtain a level surface.

uniformly moist and sticky. A few drops of water should trickle out when the compost is squeezed. Pack the tool with the compost, smooth off any excess, then press out the blocks onto a clean surface.

When you have made a few blocks, test their consistency, rejecting any that have crumbled or do not hold together (return rejects to the remaining stock, and mix in).

Place the peat blocks close to each other, but not touching, on a capillary mat (see page 34) or into seed trays. Cover them with a large opaque polythene sheet to retain the moisture and exclude bright light. Remove the sheet when the seeds have germinated and keep the blocks with their delicate seedlings moist.

Feed the plants with a balanced liquid fertiliser if necessary (after about six weeks), and plant them out when they are ready. Do not forget to water the blocks thoroughly before planting out.

Transplanting seedlings: many gardeners prefer to sow the seeds in trays first and to transplant the seedlings to the blocks later instead of pricking them out into another tray. If you use this method, slightly enlarge the hole in the block by using a small dibber, then insert the seedling and gently firm it in.

What to do with used compost

Neither loam-based nor soil-less composts should be re-used for potting. But with the addition of a balanced fertiliser, they can be used for filling terrace pots and windowboxes. They can also be used to improve the texture of garden soil – preferably in spring.

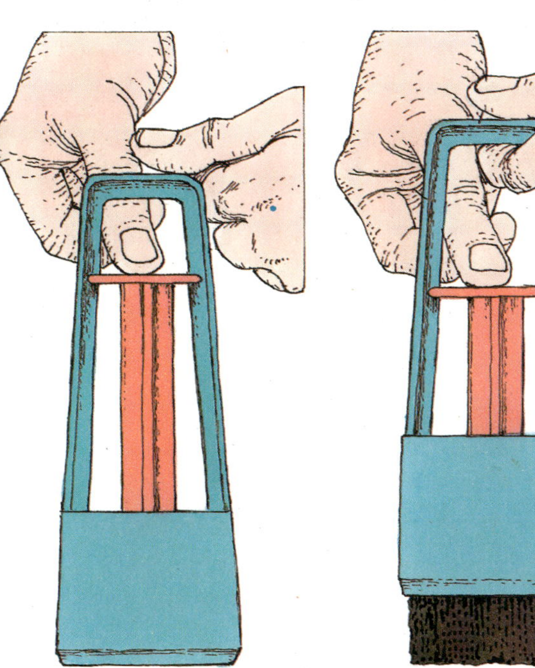

Invert the tool and depress the plunger.

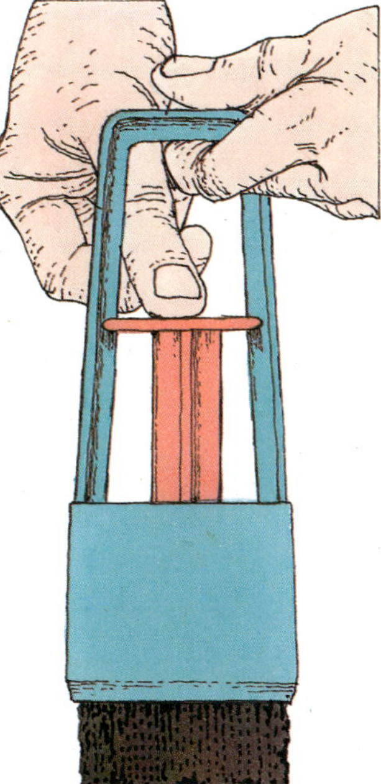

The compound is too dry if the block crumbles.

Place the blocks on a capillary mat.

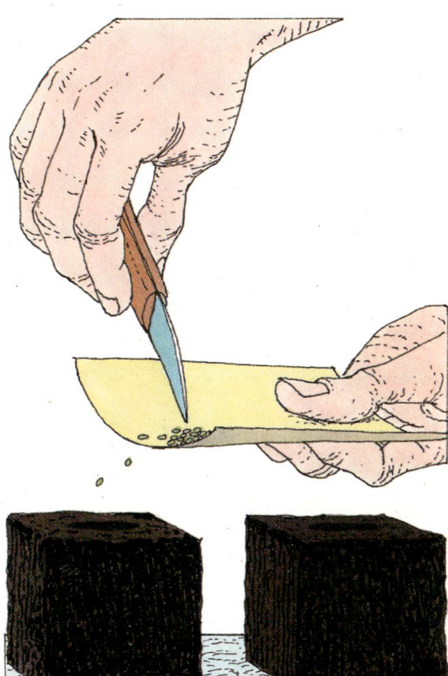

Sow seeds into the hole left by the plunger.

Enjoying your greenhouse

Although there is a whole industry eager to supply both professional and amateur gardeners with anything they may need in the plant line, in the end it is the individual grower's care that brings satisfying results. The love of plants combined with a growing understanding will soon tell the beginner what to do in the greenhouse during the course of a year.

Plants are living things. They will repay the care and attention lavished on their development: it is as if they knew the enjoyment we humans derive not only from a perfect flower, luxuriant foliage, the tang of freshly picked vegetables, but also from the intimate art of nursing young seedlings to maturity in the quiet oasis of a greenhouse.

Dealing with pests and diseases

Even professional gardeners are confronted by ailing plants from time to time, and it is inevitable that some of your plants will succumb to a pest or disease sooner or later. The key to control is to identify the pest and apply the appropriate remedy as soon as possible.

Use the tables on the following pages to identify the likely problem and to decide on a suitable control.

The chemical names used in the tables are the common chemical names. You will find this on the container, usually in small print. In some countries there may be restrictions on the sale of certain garden chemicals, but a suitable alternative is nearly always available.

The list of remedies is not exhaustive – there are many good greenfly killers, but a selection of two or three will do the job just as well and be less confusing.

The most important rule is to deal with the problem *promptly*. In the confined area of a greenhouse, fungi and insects can multiply and spread rapidly, particularly where plants are grown close together in a warm and humid atmosphere.

Having freed your plants from pests and diseases, try to keep them healthy by good greenhouse management. Keep the interior clean and tidy, and use sterilised compost and containers whenever possible.

Keep your plants well fed so that they are better able to resist attack, and only propagate from healthy stock.

CAUTION: The chemicals recommended are not in any order of preference or efficiency. Some are available in more than one formulation (dust or spray, for example), and the one given is the form recommended for the particular pest or disease.

Remember to use garden chemicals with extra caution in the confined environment of a greenhouse. Work towards the door when spraying or dusting, and do not inhale any fumes or spray. Leave to clear before working in the greenhouse.

pest:	*symptoms:*	*control:*
Ant	Familiar pest. Plants wilt due to disturbance of soil in borders, boxes or pots	Pirimiphos-methyl (dust); Pyrethrum (dust); Trichlorphon (granules)
Aphid *(greenfly/blackfly)*	Small fat green or black insect that sometimes has wings. It sucks sap, reducing vigour and stunting growth. Leaves turn yellow, curl and distort. 'Honeydew' is secreted and sooty moulds may grow on this	Pirimiphos-methyl (smoke or spray); Gamma-HCH (smoke); Pirimicarb (spray, aerosol); Rotenone (spray); Malathion (spray)
Caterpillar	Long grub, usually green. Feeds on leaves, making large holes. Usually a problem in summer	Pick off plant and destroy. Fenitrothion (spray); Rotenone (dust); Permethrin (spray); Dimethoate (systemic spray)
Cutworm	Large, fat, greyish-cream caterpillar on soil. Curls up if disturbed. Chews off plants at soil level, usually in summer and autumn	Pirimiphos-methyl (spray or dust); Carbaryl (dust) Diazinon (granules)

Earwig	Long, brown body with rear pincers. Chews holes in leaves, flower buds and florets	Gamma-HCH (spray or dust); Rotenone with carbaryl (dust); Pirimiphos-methyl (dust)
Eelworm	Minute worm-like insects that usually feed within roots. Stems and roots may be distorted, leaves discoloured	Destroy plant. Do not replant with same crop
Flea beetle	Tiny black and yellow beetle that jumps when disturbed. Adult makes holes in leaves, mainly in brassica (cabbage family) seedlings. Most likely to be troublesome in late spring or early summer	Carbaryl (dust); Gamma-HCH (dust); Rotenone (dust)
Leaf miner	Small grubs that cause silver-white winding lines, blisters or blotching of leaves. Usually noticed in summer and autumn	Gamma-HCH (spray); Malathion (spray)
Leatherjacket	Dark grey legless grub. Larva of daddy-longlegs. Feeds on roots causing plant to wilt	Carbaryl (dust); Diazinon (granules)
Mealy bug	Tiny white, waxy insect. The protective white cottony 'fluff' covering it is usually found on stems or in leaf axils	Permethrin (spray); Malathion (spray); Dimethoate (systemic spray)
Mouse/rat	Familiar pests. Seed beds disturbed, and stored seeds/bulbs eaten	Difenacoum (bait); Coumatetralyl (bait); (replenish bait regularly)
Red spider mite	Tiny red or yellow mite. Lays eggs on undersides of leaves. Sucks sap, causing motling of leaves which turn yellow or rusty brown. In severe attacks there is a white webbing between leaves and stems. Worst from spring to autumn	Permethrin (spray); Dimethoate (systemic spray); Malathion (spray); Rotenone (spray); Pirimiphos-methyl; with synergised pyrethrins (aerosol)
Root aphid	Greyish 'greenfly', found on roots. Sucks sap, causing stunted growth; leaves turn yellow and wilt. May be most troublesome in autumn and spring	Pirimiphos-methyl (spray or dust, on compost). Gamma-HCH (spray, on compost); Malathion (spray, on compost)
Scale insect	Small immobile disc-shaped brown insect. Appears as scurfy flake on stem or underneath leaf. Worst in summer	Malathion (spray); Dimethoate (systemic spray)
Slug/snail	Familiar pests. Irregular holes in leaves, stems or tubers. Telltale trails. Seedlings and mature plants attacked	Metaldehyde (bait); Methiocarb (bait)
Thrip	Minute yellow, brown or black insect. May cause speckling and streaking of leaves and flowers. Most trouble in summer and autumn	Permethrin (spray or smoke); Malathion (spray); Gamma-HCH (spray)
Vine weevil	Creamy-white grub. Feeds on roots, corms and tubers. Affected plant may wilt or even die	Gamma-HCH (spray, on compost); Carbaryl (dust, on compost)
Whitefly	Tiny, white 'triangular' insect found on undersides of leaves. Will rise in a 'cloud' and fly around in circles when disturbed. Sucks sap and secretes 'honeydew', encouraging sooty mould. A problem from spring to autumn	Malathion (spray); Permethrin (smoke); Pyrethrum with resmethrin (aerosol); Bioresmethrin (spray or aerosol)
Woodlouse	Grey, hard-coated pest that usually rolls into a ball if disturbed. Attacks seedlings and young damaged plants. May also feed on leaves, causing jagged holes	Carbaryl (dust, on compost); Gamma-HCH (dust, on compost)

Disease control table

disease or disorder	*symptoms*	*control*
Blackleg	Base of cutting blackened, rotting at ground level. Worse in winter	Destroy affected plants. Tecnazene (smoke); Copper sulphate with ammonium carbonate (spray, on compost)
Blossom end rot	Fruit develops dark patches at the bottom end. Due to irregular watering	Physiological disorder. Keep soil moist
Botrytis *(grey mould)*	Fluffy mould on stems, leaves, flowers or fruit. Tissue rots rapidly	Avoid overwatering; ventilate whenever possible. Benomyl (spray); Tecnazene (smoke)
Chlorosis	Leaves turn yellow. Usually associated with chalky soil or compost and particularly affects lime-hating plants	Sequestered iron (spray, on compost)
Damping-off	Seedlings topple over and die off	Do not overwater. Ventilate whenever possible. Copper sulphate with ammonium carbonate (spray, on compost)
Grey mould	*See Botrytis*	
Mildew	White powdery patches on leaves and shoot tips	Benomyl (spray); Mancozeb (spray); Bupirimate with triforine (systemic spray)
Root rot	Leaves turn yellow, shrivel and wilt. Roots black and rotten	Copper sulphate with ammonium carbonate (spray, on compost). Water carefully
Rust	Orange or brown powdery spots, usually on underside of leaves and stems	Destroy affected leaves. Copper compound (spray); Mancozeb (spray)
Sooty mould	Black fungus grows on sticky 'honeydew' deposited by aphids	If possible, remove by sponging leaves. Control aphids
Leaf spot	Yellow or brown patches on leaves, which may shrivel. Lower leaves often attacked first	Benomyl (spray); Thiophanate-methyl (spray); Ventilate to reduce humidity
Stem rot	Affects tomatoes, cucumbers, melons. Brown canker at base of stem. Leaves turn yellow and plant collapses	Mancozeb (spray); Benomyl (spray). Destroy badly affected plants. Sterilize greenhouse and the equipment between crops
Virus	Stunted and distorted growth. Yellow mottling and crinkling of leaves	No cure. Destroy plants
Wilt	Leaves turn yellow and shoots wilt. Brown ring can be seen when the stem is cut across	Benomyl (spray, on compost). Growing bags reduce risk

Index